Faith among Faiths

Faith among Faiths

Christian Theology and Non-Christian Religions

James L. Fredericks

PAULIST PRESS
New York/Mahwah, N.J.

The Publisher gratefully acknowledges use of the following: extracts from John Hick and Paul F. Knitter (eds.), *The Myth of Christian Uniqueness,* copyright 1987 by Orbis Books (Maryknoll, N.Y.) and 1988 by SCM Press (London). Used with permission.

Cover design by Cindy Dunne

Book design by Theresa M. Sparacio

Library of Congress Cataloging-in-Publication Data

Fredericks, James L.
Faith among faiths : Christian theology and non-Christian religions / James L. Fredericks.
    p.   cm.
    Includes bibliographical references.
    ISBN 0-8091-3893-X (alk. paper)
    1. Christianity and other religions.   2. Religious pluralism—Christianity.
I. Title.
BR127.F69   1999
261.2—dc21
                                        99-33720
                                           CIP

Published by Paulist Press
997 Macarthur Boulevard
Mahwah, New Jersey 07430

www.paulistpress.com

Printed and bound in the
United States of America

CONTENTS

CONTENTS

ACKNOWLEDGMENTS

However lonely an activity writing may be, books are in reality communal efforts to some degree. In the case of this book, thanks must go first to my colleagues and students at Loyola Marymount University in Los Angeles, with special thanks to Carol Turner for her patience and generosity. Also in Los Angeles, my appreciation goes to Dr. Havanpola Ratanasara and Ven. Karuma Dharma of the College of Buddhist Studies, Bhanti Samuhito of Wat Thai, Bhanti Piyananda of the Dharma Vijaya Buddhist Vihara, Rev. Masao Kodani of Senshin Temple, Rev. Kusala (who, like the Buddha, is neither from here nor from there), and to Mike Kerze. In Kyoto, I wish to thank Profs. Masao Abe, Dennis Hirota, Jan van Bragt, and Ryusei Takeda, as well as Rev. Graham McDonnell and Tomiko Minakuchi. I am grateful also to Mark Unno and Ken Tanaka. All of you have taught me a great deal about the value of friendships between those who follow different religious paths. My colleagues at the comparative theology seminar of the Catholic Theological Society of America have been especially helpful, especially Brad Malkowsky, Frank Clooney, Bob Schreiter, David Burrell, Paul Knitter, and Paul Griffiths. My thanks go as well to Profs. Wendy Doniger, David Tracy, Anne Carr, Langdon Gilkey, and the late Joseph Kitagawa. Finally, I wish to thank Kathleen Walsh of Paulist Press, who has been particularly helpful in shepherding this book into print.

James Fredericks
Kyoto, 1999

For Jack O'Hare and Randy Calvo

INTRODUCTION

The word *Asia* is really quite meaningless. This is one of the most lasting insights I brought back to the United States from a year spent studying in Japan and other parts of Asia. If places as different as the Philippines and Thailand, China and Indonesia are all *Asia*, let alone places like Bengal and Afghanistan, what does *Asia* mean? *Asia* was originally a word the Romans used for what is now modern Turkey and beyond. But the Romans had no idea that the "beyond" would one day stretch from the Bosporus to the South China Sea. Not only are Asian countries such as India and China vastly different in their languages and history; they are different in their religious outlooks as well.

Today this religious diversity has come into my classroom. In the theology classes I conduct at Loyola Marymount University in Los Angeles, I teach Hindus from Bengal and Confucians from the Chinese mainland. Muslims from Turkey meet and discuss issues with Jews from Israel and Buddhists from Vietnam. Also interesting is when my Muslim students from Turkey (very secularized) talk about their religious beliefs with less secularized Muslims from Egypt or Morocco: diversity is visible not only between religious traditions but within them as well.

Even more significant is the fact that increasingly my Buddhist, Confucian, Hindu, and Muslim students are Americans, born and raised in places like Sacramento and Pittsburgh. The contributions these Americans are making in my classroom are part of the legacy of the 1965 Immigration Act, which began to undo the racism institutionalized in immigration laws such as the first Chinese Exclusion Act (1882) and the Johnson Reed Act (1924), which effectively stopped immigration from Asia. In barring Asians, these laws also barred their religions. Today, however, there are Muslims in Providence, Sikhs in Chicago, Jains in Los Angeles. The United States is no longer a country of three religions (Protestant, Roman Catholic, Jewish). Today there are more Muslims than Episcopalians. In fact, there are more Muslims than Presbyterians. According to some counts, there are more Muslims than Jews. Buddhism is becoming an American religion that can be associated as much with Americans of European ancestry as Americans of Chinese, Korean, Japanese, or Vietnamese roots. Islam was brought to America by Syrian and Lebanese immigrants in the last century. Today the children of these immigrants are doing what Catholics and Jews have done for generations: trying to find a way to be American and faithful to their religious values at the same time. Also like Catholics and Jews, Muslims and Buddhists, Hindus and Jains, and others are discovering how the values and insights enshrined in their religious traditions can contribute to the common good of all Americans.

In some respects, America's new religious face is not always easy to see. In Los Angeles, the oldest Buddhist temple serving the Korean community occupies a former Masonic Hall above a storefront. One might not notice it driving past on Vermont Avenue. A Theravada Buddhist vihara (monastery) can be found in a rambling old house in a residential neighborhood across town. In San Jose, Vietnamese Buddhist monks seem to prefer tract homes. Look for mosques in old factories in Queens or a converted U-Haul dealership in Rhode Island. In New Jersey, an old YMCA building has become a Hindu temple. The same is true of a Methodist church in Minneapolis.

But this invisibility is quickly changing. The Chinese community in Southern California has built the largest Buddhist monastery outside of Asia in Hacienda Heights, near Los Angeles. Houston is the site of the new Jade Temple, also an impressive structure. Jains and Bah'ais have build large centers with eye-catching architecture in the suburbs of Chicago. The Sri Venkateswara Temple (Hindu) is in Pittsburgh. Tibetan Buddhists have built a large monastery on the Pacific Coast above San Francisco—not easy to find, but very beautiful and large scale.

Today the Muslim world is no longer somewhere else. Chicago has fifty mosques and roughly a half-million Muslims. America has been part of the Jewish Diaspora for generations. Now we are part of the Islamic, Hindu, and Buddhist diasporas as well. What will this mean for the United States? How will our new neighbors contribute to the formation of public policy in areas such as church–state relations, health care programs, and public school education? We are often told of the importance of race and ethnicity. As Americans we need to be aware of the problems and richness of our religious diversity as well. Examples of violence against religious believers need to be documented and better understood. Vandalism against Jewish synagogues and cemeteries, Catholic churches and convents still goes on. Now, joining the "Know Nothings," the American Nativist League and the Klan are the "Dotbusters," a New Jersey group that harasses Hindu women wearing the *bindi* (the red dot on the forehead).[1] The melody is familiar, only the lyrics have changed: "too many Jews, too many Catholics" has become "too many Chinese, too many Koreans, too many Indians."

Important as it may be to document intolerance, we also need to document and understand how our increased sense of religious diversity has led to new forms of interreligious cooperation and civility. Documenting how neighbors of very different religious backgrounds are living cooperatively and creatively with one another is harder to document than the shameful examples of intolerance that make it into the newspapers. But there are examples of cooperation and creativity aplenty. In Los Angeles, a Chinese temple decorated its front gates with twin swastikas, the ancient Buddhist symbol of the eternal "turning of the wheel of the Dharma." Some people in the neighborhood, ignorant of the swastika's meaning as a Buddhist symbol, were incensed. Vandalism resulted. But a group of religious leaders in Los Angeles met with the monks to learn about the swastika as a Buddhist symbol and preached on the incident at weekend services. Mutual understanding brought an end to the controversy. In another example, the Roman Catholic Archdiocese of Los Angeles and other Christian church groups, along with Muslim and Hindu organizations publicly supported a group of Chinese monks before the Los Angeles County Board of Supervisors when outrageous zoning obstacles were put up to block the building of

Hsi Lai Monastery. At the ground-breaking ceremonies for the new Islamic Center in Sharon, Massachusetts, in April 1993, the Muslim community was joined by Jews and Christians. In Fremont, California, St. Paul's United Methodist Church and the Islamic Society of the East Bay joined together to build a church and a mosque on the same property. On June 25, 1991, for the first time in the history of the House of Representatives, an Islamic imam, Siraj Wahau, opened a session with a prayer, in this case, "to Allah, the Beneficent, the Most Holy...."[2]

Some New Questions for Christians

In the summer of 1969, the world watched the "earth-rise" from the Sea of Tranquillity on their televisions. The image of the earth floating over the lunar horizon was beamed to Houston, Texas, and from there around the world almost instantaneously. In 1769, when Thomas Jefferson was still dreaming about sending an expedition to find a northwest passage linking the Missouri River with the Columbia River, no information traveled any faster than a horse. A letter took longer than six weeks to get from St. Louis to Jefferson in Monticello. Today we live in a period when a morning speech in the House of Representatives in Washington about recognizing Jerusalem as the capital of Israel leads to civil unrest in Palestine within hours.

Those who would presume that the technology that makes communication across the world more or less instantaneous is also transforming the world into a global village where everyone is increasingly like us are surely mistaken. In 1963, when William McNeill published his famous textbook on world history, his choice for a title, *The Rise of the West*, was remarkably revealing of his view of things.[3] The history of the world has led to the rise of Western civilization. The struggles of the ancient Sumerians, Egyptians, Chinese, and Indians have given way to the rise of the capitalist, democratic, technological West as the ascendant standard and norm for civilization today. McNeill could point to the fact that the last time a non-European civilization threatened Europe was the Turkish siege of Vienna in 1540. Since that time, the West has been a dominant civilization militarily, scientifically, economically, and of course technologically. The future of the world lies in becoming "western"—in emulating the West's embrace of a secular society, driven by economic liberalism and the scientific worldview.

We are beginning to see that McNeill's "rise of the West" is turning out more like E. M. Forster's *A Passage to India*. China and India, Iran and the Arab nations, whose religions have produced great civilizations of their own, are not becoming westernized. In fact, if anything, these societies are being extremely fussy about what they are willing to accept from the West. The West has grown too accustomed to thinking of Soviet-style Marxist-Leninism as the only possible alternative to an open liberal society. Some Western commentators have even hailed the collapse of the Soviet Union in 1989 as "the end of history," meaning that, with the victory of the West, the future of the world lies indisputably in its secular, individualistic, liberal values.[4]

But in time history may show that there are hugely more formidable alternatives to Western culture than that posed by Marxist-Leninism. East Asian intellectuals and political leaders such as Japan's Takeshi Umehara and Singapore's Senior Minister Lee Kuan Yew speak provocatively about a Confucian challenge to Western liberalism.[5] The West, they point out, has been spiritually exhausted by its extreme individualism. Instead of looking across the Pacific for moral leadership, these voices call for East Asians to look again to their own traditions of communitarian morality and filial piety where public duty is extolled over individual rights, loyalty to one's superior and deference to authority are valued over personal liberty. These virtues are the tenets of Confucian humanism, not the European Enlightenment. They hark back to the religious heritage of East Asia, not the Modern West. Similar voices can be found in India and the Islamic world.

The message should be clear. Religions such as Hinduism, Buddhism, Confucianism, Daoism, and Islam are ancient and highly sophisticated ways of imagining the world and the meaning of human life within the world. Like Christianity, these religious traditions have been the inspiration for the building up of great civilizations. Like Christianity, these religions equip their believers with a compelling vision of the meaning of human life and the fate of the individual. To presume that these religions will fade away before the irresistible tide of Western secularism (including its Marxist-Leninist form) is naive. Equally naive would it be for Christians to presume that as these ancient cultures become more westernized they will become more receptive to Christianity. If it is not necessary to subscribe to the outlook of Western secularism to be counted as civilized, neither is it necessary for an Arab or Malaysian to convert to Christianity in order to live a life that is spiritually rich and morally authentic.

The Pluralism Debate

Increasingly, Christians will need to stop and reflect on what this new awareness of diversity will mean for their communities and the future of their own religion. In fact, Christians are already doing this. A lively debate is under way among Christian theologians who are vitally interested in our new sense of religious diversity. At issue in this debate is nothing less than what we as Christian believers should think about non-Christian religions and their adherents, our new neighbors. At stake in this debate is the way Christians will respond to their neighbors who gather for worship in mosques and viharas, in gunawaras and temples, and of course synagogues as well. Perhaps most important of all, at issue here is how Christians will come to understand themselves and their own religion in new ways as a result of their encounter with their non-Christian neighbors.

Up until now, the debate has been centered on the problem of an adequate "theology of religions." A theology of religions is a Christian interpretation of the role played by non-Christian religions in the drama of salvation. In order to be saved, does a person have to have faith in Jesus Christ? Is Jesus Christ the one and only savior of the world? If Hindu believers can be saved, are they saved despite their Hindu religion or by means of their religion? If Christians think Buddhists, by worshiping the Buddha, can come to experience the grace of God in their lives, should it matter to Christians that Buddhists do not, in fact, claim to worship the Buddha?

Generally speaking, the various efforts at a workable theology of religions have concerned themselves with questions like these, which have to do with how exclusive or inclusive Christians should be about who shares in the banquet of Christ's salvation and who does not. "Exclusivists" are Christian theologians who argue that all salvation requires an explicit faith in Jesus Christ. Since this is the case, believers who follow religious paths other than the way preached by Christ cannot be saved. "Inclusivists" are theologians who believe that all salvation is through Jesus Christ, the only savior of the world, but the saving grace of Christ touches human beings who are not baptized Christians. Some of these "inclusivist theologians" argue that the saving grace of Christ actually reaches human beings through religions like Buddhism and Daoism. Therefore, non-Christians must be included among those saved because of their implicit faith in Jesus.

At the center of the debate over religious diversity is a group of scholars who are championing what they call a "pluralistic" theology of religions. Thinkers associated with the pluralistic approach, such as John Hick, Paul Knitter, Stanley Samartha and Wilfred Cantwell Smith, each take a different approach to the problem of religious diversity, but generally they are in agreement on this much: within the universe of faiths, there are many ways to salvation. The way of Christ is one path; the way of the Buddha is another. The pluralistic theology of religions differs from exclusivism in its claim that non-Christians can be saved. This approach differs from inclusivism in its claim that not all salvation is in Christ.

In opposing exclusivism and inclusivism, pluralists are required to broaden considerably the meaning of the word *salvation*. Both exclusivists and inclusivists, although they differ on how widely available salvation is, are in agreement that all salvation is found through faith in Jesus Christ. Faith in Christ gives one a share in resurrection from the dead, which leads to everlasting life in the banquet of heaven. Since both exclusivists and inclusivists agree that all salvation is in Jesus Christ, their understanding of salvation remains rooted in the traditional images supplied by the Christian tradition: the resurrection of the body, the beatific vision, justification before the Lord, the restoration of lost innocence, being an heir to the kingdom of God. Pluralists, on the other hand, claim that all religions lead to salvation, but not merely the salvation imagined by Christians. This is why pluralists have been required to expand their understanding of salvation. John Hick, to take one prominent example of a pluralist thinker, goes beyond traditional Christian images to the notion of a fundamental transformation of our human existence. This transformation, which is available through all the great religious traditions, is spoken of variously as eternal life in heaven (Christianity), as the annihilation of the illusion of separateness (Theravada Buddhism), as the unity of the soul with Brahman (Hinduism), and so on. Hick argues that all religions hold up the possibility of a "limitlessly better state," which arrives when we move away from egocentric living to a life that is "reality-centered."[6]

This expansion of the meaning of the term *salvation* means that Christians who would be open to the truths enshrined in non-Christian religions should abandon Christianity's traditional claims about the uniqueness and necessity of Christ for salvation. This book will examine this issue and some of the other important ramifications that the pluralist view of religious diversity holds for Christianity. The pluralist theology of religions has been met with a storm of protest from many sides. Some of the critics have called for a return to traditional forms of exclusivism and inclusivism. Others have tried to respond to the pluralist approach with more sophisticated forms of exclusivism and inclusivism. The critics of the pluralist approach will also be given a hearing in this book.

Currently, the quest for an adequate theology of religions is at an impasse. By *adequate* I mean a theology of religions that assists Christians in living responsibly and creatively with the intrusive fact of religious diversity we have been discussing. In addressing religious diversity, Christians need to be responsible to the demands their religious tradition places on them. At the same time, Christians should respond creatively to the enormous opportunity that religious diversity offers to Christians to think about their own religious tradition in new ways today. By *impasse* I mean that the proponents of the pluralistic approach have been very successful in exposing the inadequacies of more traditional views of Christianity in relation to other religions, but, at the same time, their critics have also been successful in exposing the inadequacies of the pluralists. In this book, I wish to recommend comparative theology as a way to get beyond this impasse.

Since *comparative theology* is not yet a term that is widely used among Christians, a few words of explanation are in order. My interest in comparative theology is based on my belief that it is no longer possible for Christians to give an adequate and completely satisfying account of the relationship between their religion and the other great religious paths. The Christian theology of religions is in a crisis today, in no small part because Buddhists and Hindus, Confucians and Muslims are no longer exotic Hollywood stereotypes. They live down the street. They work in the office next to ours. When tested by the real religious lives of these non-Christians, none of the three basic options for a theology of religions is fully adequate to the needs of Christians in this religiously diverse age. The lion's share of this book will be devoted to showing why this is so. But I also want to show how we might find a way beyond this impasse by looking to comparative theology. The last two chapters will thus be devoted to a discussion of how Christians can take religious diversity seriously by exploring their own religious tradition in dialogue with other religious traditions.

Comparative theology is not another theology of religions. All theologies of religions, be they of the exclusivist, inclusivist, or pluralist variety, are theoretical approaches to religious diversity. They think of religious diversity as a theoretical problem to be solved. Comparative theology, in contrast, is a process or practice, not a theory. Before Christians can fully understand themselves and the role of their religion in the history of the world's many religions, we must first learn *about* non-Christians. Even then, the job of comparative theology has only begun. After learning *about* non-Christians and their religions, we will then ready to learn *from* them.

Once Christians begin to take the truths of non-Christian religions seriously, we should not expect that their faith will be left untouched. An encounter in depth with a religion not our own can be frightening and confusing. Coming face to face with views of life and death, good and evil that are so very *different* from our own can be destabilizing. But such encounters can be life giving as well. The truths of non-Christian religions can stimulate Christians to look into their own religious tradition with new questions and emerge, perhaps, with new insights. Comparative theology may lead Christians to see the challenge posed by their non-Christian neighbors not as a threat, but as a blessing in the deepest sense of the word.

Here, then, is yet another reason that our response to religious diversity needs to be not only responsible to the legacy of our religious tradition but also creative in interpreting the tradition in new and innovative ways in the light of our new appreciation of religious diversity. In order to be creative in responding to non-Christians and in understanding our own faith anew, we should stop theorizing about non-Christian religions and start learning about them. By learning about them we will place ourselves in a position to begin learning from them. The process of exploring Christianity, guided, stimulated, empowered by the questions and insights of a non-Christian religion, is to do Christian theology comparatively. In comparative theology, Christians will find a way beyond the current impasse in the theology of religions.

This book, then, has two purposes. First, I want to summarize the lively debate that is currently under way regarding the pluralistic theology of religions. In addition, I want to suggest comparative theology as an alternative to the theology of religions and a way to get beyond the current impasse over the pluralistic model.

The first chapter of the book is given to setting the scene for the contemporary debate on pluralistic theology of religions. I have chosen the two theologians most clearly associated with the exclusivist and inclusivist models for the theology of religions, Karl Barth and Karl Rahner. The second, third, and fourth chapters examine prominent examples of the pluralistic theology of religions, John Hick, Paul Knitter, Stanley Samartha, and Wilfred Cantwell Smith. I hope to show that there is a healthy pluralism among the pluralists and that pluralist theologians have changed their minds and amended their views considerably as a result of the continuing debate. The fifth and six chapters are intended to give the critics of the pluralist theologians a hearing. The seventh and eighth chapters are about comparative theology as an alternative to the three candidates for a theology of religions. In chapter seven, I offer two examples of doing theology comparatively. In the first example, I compare a Hindu story about Krishna with Jesus' parable of the Prodigal Son. In the second example, I use the thought of Dogen, one of the founders of Zen Buddhism in Japan, to explore the meaning of the resurrection for Christians. The eighth chapter reflects on the whole process of doing theology comparatively.

Today, most participants in the debate over an adequate theology of religions would agree that the discussion has come to an impasse. Fundamental differences have come to the surface and been clarified, but not resolved. A small but growing number of Christian theologians are beginning to study the teachings and practices of non-Christians religions seriously. These theologians are also beginning to return to their own religious tradition with new insights and new questions. They are beginning to think about Christianity in new and exciting ways and to share their insights with the larger Christian community. Theologians like Francis X. Clooney, John B. Cobb, Don Mitchell, David Burrell, and John Keenan are no longer engaged in the quest for an adequate theology of religions. They are doing theology comparatively. Here lies a way beyond the impasse in the theology of religions.

NOTES

1. Diana Eck, "The Mosque Next Door," *Harvard Magazine*, Sept.-Oct. 1996, p. 43.

2. For accounts such as these, see Diana Eck, *Encountering God: A Spiritual Journey from Bozeman to Banaras* (Boston: Beacon Press, 1993).

3. William McNeill, *The Rise of the West* (Chicago: University of Chicago Press, 1991).

4. See Francis Fukuyama, *The End of History and the Last Man* (New York: Free Press, 1992); idem, *Have We Reached the End of History?* (Santa Monica, Calif.: Rand Corporation, 1989).

5. See, for example, Lee Kuan Yew, "Looking East: The Confucian Challenge to Western Liberalism," *New Perspectives Quarterly* 9, no. 1 (Winter 1992).

6. See John Hick, *An Interpretation of Religion: Human Responses to the Transcendent (*New Haven: Yale University Press, 1989), 21–55.

Chapter 1

BEFORE PLURALISM

A theology of religions offers an interpretation for Christians of the meaning of non-Christian religions and their role, if any, in the salvation of the world. There is nothing new about this issue within Christian theology. Christians have been confronted with the need to make sense out of non-Christian religions since the very earliest days of the Christian movement. Today, however, this ancient task has taken on a new urgency and excitement. This chapter deals with the discussion among theologians about religious diversity, which led up to the current debate over pluralism.

A Theology of Religions

Generally speaking, any theology of religions must deal with two traditional Christian affirmations. First, Christians have claimed that Jesus is the incarnation of God within human history, the unique savior of the world. But in addition to this affirmation, Christians have also held that God wills to save all human beings. The uniqueness of Jesus and the universality of God's will to save: every theology of religions must somehow make sense of these two Christian truths.

There is no shortage of support for both affirmations in the Bible. When the uniqueness of Jesus as sole savior of the world is under discussion, the passage in the fourth chapter of the Acts of the Apostles comes readily to mind. Peter, about to enter the temple in Jerusalem

13

with John, has cured a crippled beggar with the words, "in the name of Jesus Christ the Nazorean, [rise and] walk" (Acts 3:6). The commotion caused by this cure eventually brings Peter before the Jewish leadership in Jerusalem. They demand that Peter tell them, "by what power or by what name" he has worked the miracle. Peter answers,

> ...all of you and all the people of Israel should know that it was in the name of Jesus Christ the Nazorean whom you crucified, whom God raised from the dead; in his name this man stands before you healed. He is "the stone rejected by you, the builders, which has become the cornerstone." There is no salvation through anyone else, nor is there any other name under heaven given to the human race by which we are to be saved. (Acts 4:10–12)

In the same book of the Bible, we also find support for Christian belief in the universality of God's will to save all human beings. While in Athens, the apostle Paul spoke the following words in the Areopagus (a public square),

> You Athenians, I see that in every respect you are very religious. For as I walked around looking carefully at your shrines, I even discovered an altar inscribed, "To an Unknown God." What therefore you unknowingly worship, I proclaim to you. (Acts 17:22–23)

Paul is recognizing the possibility that non-Christians may be worshiping the God of Jesus Christ without knowing it. Implied in this is the view that a human being need not have an explicit faith in Jesus Christ in order to know the God revealed by Jesus Christ. Non-Christians may be included in the salvation witnessed to by Christians.

Every theology of religions must come to terms with the necessity of faith in Jesus Christ for salvation and the universality of God's offer of salvation. How are these two Christian teachings to be related to each other? Are they incompatible? Can they be reconciled? All theologies of religions hold these two affirmations together in one way or another. Recently, we have come to think of all the candidates for an adequate theology of religions as falling into one of three types: exclusivism, inclusivism, or pluralism.[1] Exclusivist theologies of religion claim that Christianity is the only true religion. No other religious path is founded on Jesus Christ, the unique and unsurpassable savior of the world. God's salvation is available to all, but only through Jesus Christ. Inclusivist theologies are in agreement with exclusivist theologies in claiming that all salvation is in the name of Jesus Christ. But these theologies also argue that God's saving grace is present universally and therefore no human being is untouched by the grace of the God revealed by Jesus Christ. Salvation outside the institutional borders of Christianity is a distinct possibility. Non-Christians are included, at least potentially, in the salvation enjoyed by Christians.

Pluralistic theologies of religion go beyond inclusivist theologies in their willingness to recognize the possibility of salvation apart from Christianity. For the pluralist theologians, Christ is one way to salvation, but not the only way. Buddhism constitutes another religious path that leads to salvation. The same can be said for the religions of the Muslims and Sikhs and the followers of the other great traditions. Inclusivists believe that Christ is at work in the souls of non-Christian believers. The pluralists claim that non-Christian religions are legitimate ways to salvation apart from the way of Christ. Therefore as a general rule, pluralistic theologies are willing to abandon the traditional Christian belief in Christ as the one and only savior. There are many ways to reach the top of the mountain. The way of Christ is but one of those ways. There is nothing superior about Christianity.

These three types, exclusivism, inclusivism, and pluralism, are rough classifications only, not strict definitions. Within each classification there exists a wide range of differences and nuances. For example, among exclusivist theologies, some hold that non-Christian religions are evil, while others believe that they are (merely) beautiful reflections of human genius (and thus not sources of God's saving grace). Inclusivist theologies are also not in agreement on the role played by non-Christian religions in the salvation of their adherents. Some inclusivist theologians believe that non-Christians can be saved despite their religious commitments, while others think they are saved by means of those religious commitments.

The debate over the pluralistic model for a theology of religions began in the 1980s with the works of theologians such as John Hick and Paul Knitter. Their works and those of other pluralists will be examined in due time. The roots of the debate over pluralism go back to earlier discussions among Christians about exclusivism and inclusivism. This is where the discussion of pluralism must start.

No Other Name but Jesus

Some will no doubt want to associate the exclusivist theology of religions with examples of Christian narrow-mindedness and intolerance toward the non-Christian "heathens." This would be a mistake. Many exclusivist theologians are articulate and carefully measured in their conclusions, including the leading example of an exclusivist theology, Karl Barth. In his monumental work, *Church Dogmatics*,[2] Barth makes four basic points to defend his belief that non-Christian faiths do not lead to salvation.

Barth's first point has to do with revelation. Revelation is God's sovereign self-manifestation.[3] In revealing himself, God is not under any compulsion or in compliance with any requirement imposed on him. For this reason, when human beings are confronted with the self-manifestation of the living God, they realize that God and God alone is the sovereign Lord over all creation. As the Creator, God owes nothing to anyone. In revelation, the complete freedom and sovereignty of God dawn on human beings as an utterly unprecedented truth that cannot be fully explained or predicted by any form of human philosophy, a truth that cannot be known apart from God's free decision to reveal himself.

In addition to the realization of God's awesome sovereignty, through God's revelation human beings come to understand their own powerlessness and sinfulness. In revelation, we are struck by the truth that we are incapable of saving ourselves by means of our own wisdom, energy, ingenuity, or strength. For all our technological genius, our entrepreneurial efforts and political skill, left to ourselves we are doomed, helpless before our own self-destructive impulses. For this reason, our only hope lies in God's unmerited love, which is bestowed on us through Jesus Christ, God's final, unsurpassable revelation within the history of the human race.

God's revelation in Jesus Christ does not fulfill our previous attempts to save ourselves. The grace of God in Jesus does not complete the plans and projects that human beings have already started. God's self-manifestation through Jesus Christ does not "fit in" with human philosophy to complete what was still partial. Revelation replaces all of our attempts to save ourselves, "putting them in the shadows to which they belong." For this reason, God's revelation brings us to the understanding that salvation is always in the name of Jesus Christ alone. There is "no other name."

> The revelation of God in Jesus Christ maintains that our justification and sanctification, our conversion and salvation, have been brought about and achieved once and for all in Jesus Christ. And our faith in Jesus Christ consists in our recognizing and admitting and affirming and accepting the fact that everything has actually been done for us once and for all in Jesus Christ. He is the assistance that comes to us. He alone is the Word of God that is spoken to us.[4]

All of our attempts to know God from our own standpoint, based on human powers of reason or mystical intuition, are wholly and entirely futile.[5] Revelation captures us off guard and exposes all our life projects as no more than schemes by which we attempt to deny our powerlessness over death and to cover over our guilt with an aura of respectability.

Barth's second point has to do with the implications of his understanding of revelation for our understanding of what a religion is. If Jesus Christ is God's free self-manifestation, utterly undeserved and unprecedented, if human wisdom cannot approximate the astounding newness of God's revelation, then there can be no knowledge of God apart from his special revelation within history: Jesus Christ. What then of the devotion of the Hindus, the renunciation of the Buddhists? What are Christians to say of the submission (*islami*) of the Muslims? Do the great religions of the world lead us to a knowledge of God? In Barth's view, religions, all religions without exception, are merely human creations. They offer only one example after another of our foolish, sinful attempts to justify ourselves apart from the grace of God.

Religions are human attempts to do what God alone has done for sinful human beings in Jesus Christ. Worse still, religions offer human beings a way to bolt and bar the door against revelation. Or in Barth's memorable word, religion is "unbelief."[6] The religions of the world are all attempts to keep at bay the Word of God, which judges but also saves, and to substitute for it a false wisdom of merely human manufacture. For this reason, religion is "a concern, indeed we must say that it is the one great concern, of godless man."[7] Religion is a lie flung from the mouth of human beings. Revelation is the unassailable truth of God. In religion, the human voice attempts to drown out the voice of God. In revelation, it is God and God alone who speaks.

Barth does not believe that religion cooperates with revelation. In fact, the two are antagonistic. The Word of God does not exist in the world and become accessible to human beings in the form of religious teachings and practices. God does not reach out to his creatures through the religions. Thus religions, cannot serve as a medium for revelation. Most shocking of all, Barth thinks of revelation as the abolition of religion. In revelation, religious paths are contradicted and exposed as forms of unbelief. The *satori* of a Zen Buddhist and the ecstasy of a Muslim Dervish tell us nothing about God. The poetry of the *Baghavad Gita* and the ethics of the Confucian *Analects* reflect merely human wisdom. Moreover, these human achievements are ways that human beings have devised for hiding from the living God. Of course the abolition of religion by revelation cannot be demonstrated by using sociology or psychology or anthropology. This truth is known only in the light of God's final, unsurpassable, religion-shattering self-revelation in Jesus Christ.[8]

As a religion, revelation exposes Christianity as well as a form of unbelief.[9] This marks Barth's third point. The goal of his theology of revelation and his indictment of religions is not to promote Christianity as a superior religion. Christianity too is merely a human creation, and thus also to be counted an expression of the rebellion of the creature against the sovereign will of the Creator. For this reason, Barth warns his readers that Christians must always speak about non-Christians with tolerance.[10]

Moreover, the tolerance that Christians show to non-Christians and their religions is not the condescension of one who knows his religion is superior. Neither is Christian tolerance an example of the self-control exercised by someone holding all the aces. The tolerance called for on the part of Christians in dealing with non-Christians is based in the "forbearance of Christ" in the face of our continued rebellion against God. Christians understand that God has reconciled himself to sinful human beings through the death and resurrection of Jesus Christ.[11] Therefore the judgment that religions are "unbelief" is not the Christian believer's assessment of non-Christian religions, but rather God's judgment on all religions, including Christianity. The Christian, as much as any Muslim, Hindu, or Jew, is humbled before the majesty of revelation.

In Barth's fourth point, however, he seems to take back with one hand what he has just given away with the other. Christianity may be "unbelief" like all the other religions, but at the same time it must be seen as the only "true religion."[12] God has decided, for his own reasons, to reveal himself to the world through the Christian church. Thus, we can speak of Christianity as the "true religion" but only in the sense that Martin Luther could speak of a "justified sinner." Since God has saved sinners from their own self-destructive sinfulness, they cannot claim any virtue for themselves. Similarly, Christianity, despite the fact that it is yet another form of our refusal to trust in God, has been chosen by God for the salvation of all. Christianity has been made true by the grace of God and cannot claim any innate superiority over other religions for being true. Christianity has no "inward worthiness" or "any immanent rightness or holiness" of its own.[13] Presumably God could have chosen any religion and made it the one true religion. Once this major qualification is acknowledged, Barth notes that "we need have no hesitation in saying that Christianity is the true religion."

These four points, gleaned from Barth's discussion of revelation and religion in *Church Dogmatics*, lead to an inescapable conclusion. Only those who profess faith in Jesus Christ, the final and unsurpassable revelation of God to the world, can be saved.

Faithful to the Tradition?

In order for a theology of religions to be adequate to the needs of Christians today, it must equip us for dealing both responsibly and creatively with the intrusive fact of religious diversity. In living well with their non-Christian neighbors, Christians must be responsible to the demands of the Christian tradition regarding the uniqueness of

Jesus Christ in the salvation of the world as well as the universality of God's will to save. In addition, Christians must be creative in their willingness to understand their tradition in new ways as a result of what they have learned from their non-Christian neighbors.

Does Barth's exclusivist theology of religions measure up to this standard? Is it in keeping with the Christian tradition? Does it empower Christians to live creatively with non-Christians? Does it invite Christians to learn more about their non-Christian neighbors? Does it suggest ways in which Christians might begin to learn from their neighbors in order to deepen their understanding of their own religious beliefs?

In regard to Barth's fidelity to the Christian tradition, he can certainly appeal to passages in the Bible to support his views. However, the Bible's support of exclusivism is ambiguous at best. The New Testament does claim that salvation is through "no other name." But there are also passages that affirm God's will to save every human being. In addition to Paul's speech to the Athenians cited above, this theme can also be found in 1 Timothy 2:4 and Romans 2:6–7. In fact, the New Testament contains ample support for the two basic Christian doctrines that affect the theology of religions. First, the scriptures affirm the necessity of faith in Jesus Christ to be saved. Second, they also affirm that God's saving love touches every human being. Exclusivist theologies generally emphasize the former at the expense of the latter. Barth's exclusivist approach does not do justice to the fullness of the Christian tradition. The God preached by Jesus of Nazareth and witnessed to in the New Testament is not indifferent or even hostile to the vast majority of the human race.

Barth's tendency to emphasize some Bible passages at the expense of others is not the only problem of his exclusivism in relation to the Christian tradition. A second problem with finding support for this exclusivism in the Christian tradition lies in its understanding of sin and damnation. In theologies that restrict salvation to Christians alone, it would seem that non-Christians are damned not by any free act of their own but by quirk of fate. Christianity teaches that all human beings suffer because of sin and are in need of God's grace to be redeemed from their predicament. The problem with exclusivist theologies such as Barth's is that the predicament of some people (non-Christians) is significantly worse than that of others (Christians). Those who have heard the gospel can be damned only to the extent that they freely choose to reject God's love. Non-Christians have not heard the gospel and are damned not by their free choice but by the historical accident of their birth as non-Christians. Fate, not the freedom to reject the good news of the gospel, leads to their eternal damnation. In this fashion, exclusivist theologies establish a double standard for salvation: only a tiny minority of human beings have received the opportunity to respond to God's grace in freedom; everyone else is damned without a choice.[14]

Helpful for Believers?

The second test for an adequate theology of religions has to do with the need for Christians to live creatively with their non-Christian neighbors. Is Barth's exclusivism helpful in this regard? Here as well, exclusivism does not seem adequate to the challenge facing Christians today.

Exclusivists need to be asked, for instance, how they know that the religious lives of non-Christians are meaningless. In an interview that has since become widely reported, Karl Barth was asked how he knew that Hinduism was a form of unbelief, given the fact that he had never met a Hindu. Barth's answer pushes us back on our heels. Hinduism can be known to be unbelief, according to Barth, a priori.[15] Without studying the Vedas and the Upanishads, without knowing anything about the *avatars* of Vishnu or the multiple manifestations of Shiva, Christian believers must judge Hinduism to be an expression of the creature's rebellion against the Creator.

Can Christians come to credible conclusions about non-Christians and their religions without knowing something about these religions? Barth tries eliminate this need to learn about other religions by taking as his starting point his radical distinction between religion (a purely human creation) and revelation (an utterly unprecedented intervention by God into the life of a human being). But this approach presupposes at the beginning what needs to be proved. Is the non-Christian completely benighted and wholly ignorant of God? This should be the conclusion of an exclusivist theology of religions, not its starting point.

For example, several observers have pointed out the remarkable similarities between the Pure Land Buddhist teachings and Christian teachings about grace.[16] A Japanese Buddhist like Shinran (1173–1262) and a Christian like Martin Luther both held that human beings can be saved from their sinfulness by grace alone. Yet Barth thinks that he can conclude that Buddhism is unbelief without having to learn anything about Buddhism. Buddhists merely talk about grace. Christians have grace because God has willed it so through Jesus Christ. "Only one thing is really decisive for the distinction of truth and error…That one thing is the name of Jesus Christ…which alone constitutes the truth of our religion."[17] To claim that there is a difference between merely talking about grace (as Pure Land Buddhists do) and the reality of grace (which the Christian enjoys) ignores an important question, that is, What is it about the religious lives of Pure Land Buddhists that leads them to talk about grace in a manner so similar to the way Luther does? Barth's extreme distinction between revelation and religion safely protects him from the need to learn about non-Christian religions.

If Barth's distinction between religion and revelation excuses Christians from the need to learn *about* their non-Christian neighbors, it also lures Christians away from the opportunity to learn *from* non-Christians. This being the case, exclusivist theologies should be judged a missed opportunity for Christians. At the heart of the problem is Barth's claim that religion and revelation are two utterly different things. How would our view of non-Christian religions change if we denied what Barth asserts? What if God chose to reveal himself through human symbols? What if we thought of revelation as the fulfillment of a universally human religious quest? In this case, contrary to Karl Barth, revelation could never be abstracted from its many religious expressions. In religions, the human quest to know God and to be transformed by grace would intermingle with God's desire to save every human being. Such a view of religion would lead to an inclusivist theology of religions.

Nostra Aetate

Barth's exclusivist approach to religious diversity hardly exhausts the options available to Christians for a theology of religions. The exclu-

22

sivist approach tends to be favored by evangelical Protestant Christians. Roman Catholics and mainline Protestants, on the other hand, tend to subscribe more to an inclusivist approach. Inclusivist theologies, like exclusivist theologies, insist that all salvation is through Jesus Christ. But unlike exclusivism, inclusivism is willing to recognize that the saving grace of Christ is at work outside of the boundaries of the institutional church. Thus, although they do not acknowledge Christ to be the savior explicitly, Hindus and Muslims, Daoists and Sikhs are not strangers to the Holy Spirit and must be counted, at least potentially, among the saved.

Examples of Protestant inclusivist theologians are by no means hard to come by. J. N. Farquar, a Protestant missionary who spent years in India, claimed that Christ was the "crown of Hinduism" and that the highest spiritual aspirations of the people of India were to be found in Christ. John Wesley himself, who with his brother Charles founded Methodism, counseled his followers to leave the question of who is damned to God—the God who is God for non-Christians as well as for Christians.

The greatest example of inclusivism in recent times was the Vatican II document entitled "The Declaration on the Relation of the Church to Non-Christian Religions," more commonly known by the first two words of the original Latin version of the document, *Nostra Aetate*. In this document, the Roman Catholic Church officially teaches that individual religions are to be praised for the way they have responded to "those profound mysteries of the human condition." Hinduism, Buddhism, and Islam all contain "the truth that enlightens every human being." After praising the various religions for their impressive achievements, *Nostra Aetate* continues with a much-quoted passage.

> The Catholic Church rejects nothing which is true and holy in these religions. She looks with sincere respect upon those ways of conduct and of life, those rules and teachings which, though differing in many particulars from what she holds and sets forth, nevertheless often reflect a ray of that Truth which enlightens all men.[18]

This passage is often quoted as a breakthrough in Christian thinking about other religions. And rightly so. Herein lies the basis for an inclusivist theology of religions. Christians, if they will look into the religious teachings and customs of the great religions of the world, will find there a ray of the truth that enlightens all.

But this passage also carries with it a real ambiguity. Nowhere in *Nostra Aetate* is it claimed that Hinduism, Buddhism, Islam, or the other great religious traditions are ways of salvation. Nowhere is this view denied. Thus, a more cautious reading of the document would hold that individual non-Christian believers can be saved *despite* their religious tradition. On the other hand, a "loose constructionist" might read the document to mean that Hinduism and Buddhism, Daoism and Confucianism as *religious paths distinct from Christianity* make available to their believers the saving grace of Christ.

The Anonymous Christian

Nostra Aetate would never have been possible were it not for Karl Rahner, S.J., the great champion of Roman Catholic inclusivism. In his resolve to assist his church in its dialogue with the modern world, Rahner must be counted among the greatest of Roman Catholic theologians of the twentieth century. A major aspect of the modern world for Rahner was the reality of non-Christians and their religious traditions. Rahner's inclusivist theology, what he called the "theology of the anonymous Christian," was at the same time one of his most controversial contributions to contemporary theology.

Rahner's theology of the anonymous Christian was developed in a number of articles published over several years and amended somewhat in response to his critics. His inclusivist approach to religious diversity can be summarized in four statements.[19]

First, Christianity must be distinguished from other religions as the "absolute religion." God intended the church to be the religious home for every human being. Since Christianity proclaims Jesus as the Christ, God's final and unsurpassable revelation to the world, no other religion can claim to speak with the same authority as Christianity. Christ is the unique incarnation of the Word of God come into the world, and the church is Christ's continuing historical presence in the world today. However, even though Christianity must be seen as "absolute," this exalted status has a complex history. There was a time before the birth of Jesus of Nazareth and the foundation of the church. In these ancient days, there were forms of Buddhism, Daoism, Confucianism, and Hinduism. Certainly there was the faith of Israel. Before all of these religious traditions, there were the tribal religions. These religions cannot be without significance in the eyes of God. In addition, today there are people who have not yet had the opportunity to hear the message of Jesus preached to them and to respond to that message out of the depths of their own freedom as religious persons. For example, a peasant on the Tibetan plateau clings to her Buddhist faith as a source of hope and cultural dignity. She has not heard the gospel in any meaningful way. Certainly, conversion to the gospel and baptism into the church are not real options for her. Christianity may be the "absolute religion" in a general and theoretical way, but the import of this statement for a particular individual depends entirely on that person's actual historical circumstances.

From this point Rahner draws two conclusions. First, Rahner believes that Christianity's call to conversion becomes obligatory or binding only when an individual is ready to hear the good news of the gospel and respond to it in freedom. Until that time, Christianity may be the absolute religion theoretically, but not in any concrete way. Second, the fact that the church's mission to spread the gospel to all peoples has a history means that a non-Christian religion is not necessarily made obsolete with the coming of the Christian church. God may have intended some religions to comfort and inspire a people until they are able to hear the Gospel and be converted to the way of Christ. Thus, to be a non-Christian today does not mean automatically that someone has actually rejected Christianity.

Rahner's second statement has to do with the role played by non-Christian religions in God's overall plan of salvation. The religion of a non-Christian believer should not be considered merely a natural form of wisdom. Religions like Daoism and Hinduism may be considered supernatural revelations intended by God for the salvation of the world. This second statement by Rahner must be contrasted dramatically with Barth's claim that religions are "unbelief."

In Rahner's view, non-Christian religions are not merely products of human creativity. God has chosen to be revealed through them. Barth claimed that there was no such thing as a "natural theology" in which human beings come to a real knowledge of God based on their own innate power to reflect on the wonder of creation and the experience of love and freedom. Apart from hearing the gospel of Jesus Christ proclaimed, human beings remain in ignorance of the saving name of Jesus. Roman Catholics have traditionally claimed that a "natural" knowledge of God was possible for all human beings no matter who they were. God is revealed to individuals in the grandeur of creation, in selfless acts of love, in the renunciation of violence—whether or not the individuals in question are baptized. Rahner goes beyond this traditional Roman Catholic belief. The experience of the living God that comes from the mysticism of the Sufis and the devotionalism of the Hindus is not merely a "natural" knowledge of God, as if this knowledge was merely the result of the effort of the individual. The Muslim and the Hindu, and for that matter the Confucian, the Buddhist, and others, enjoy a "supernatural revelation" in which God has specifically willed to enter into the life of the non-Christian believer.[20]

Based on this interpretation of God's universal will to save and the universal human quest for transcendence, Rahner was led to a daring conclusion. God saves human beings *through* the non-Christian religions, not *despite* them. Buddhists and Muslims do not come into contact with the grace of Christ in purely interior ways, unrelated to their concrete lives as believing and practicing Muslims and Buddhists. The infinitely loving God who created Christianity has also created Islam and Buddhism in order to save Muslims and Buddhists. Thus non-Christian religions, potentially at least, are ways that lead to the same salvation enjoyed by Christians. In the end, non-Christian believers will share in the heavenly banquet and the communion of the saints.[21]

Rahner's third and fourth statements draw out the implications of his first two statements. Both statements have to do with the way Christians deal with their non-Christian neighbors. In his third statement, Rahner notes that when Christians deal with non-Christians, they are not dealing with people who are strangers to the saving grace of God. Because of the universality of grace, Christians must look upon Sikhs and Daoists as Christians, or more precisely, as Christians "without the name," that is to say, as "anonymous Christians."[22] To say otherwise would be to imply that Christianity has a monopoly on God's revelation to the world. In the *ahimsa* (nonviolence) of the Jain and the *karuna* (compassion) of the Buddhist, Jains and Buddhists are transformed by the saving grace of Jesus Christ. They cannot be said to be utter strangers to the church. They are Christians, but anonymously so.

Rahner's fourth statement is about the church. If non-Christians are actually anonymous Christians, what is the purpose of the Christian missionary effort to convert people to Christianity? If salvation is available to a Hindu through Hinduism, why should a Hindu become a Christian? Has Rahner not undermined the basis for evangelization?

Rahner readily admitted that his inclusivist theology calls for a reevaluation of the church's role in the world, especially in terms of its missionary effort. The theology of the anonymous Christian is not intended to undercut the church's missionary effort. Christianity remains the "absolute religion" intended for all human beings. The inclusivist approach, however, does help to protect Christians from the sin of pride. Christians need to remember that the salvation of the world is the work of Christ, not any achievement of the church. The church is but a little leaven in the dough of God's overall plan of salvation.

Yet the church is not to be dismissed. The Christian community is the "historical vanguard" of the kingdom of God and the explicit witness to the coming of the kingdom of God that, however, cannot be restricted to the church.[23] Rahner believed that the theology of the anonymous Christian should be seen as humility on the part of Christians, not presumption. Taking an inclusivist approach to the problem of religious diversity allows God to be greater than the church.

Barth and Rahner

Rahner's theology of the anonymous Christian was not only an attempt to respond pastorally to the fact of religious diversity. Rahner was led to his inclusivist theology by his deepest convictions about God and his Christian vision of what it means to be human. The same can be said of Barth's exclusivist theology of religions. In this respect, when we look to the differing visions of Christian faith that inspired

Barth and Rahner, their different approaches to the theology of religions can be contrasted in some dramatic ways.

First, Rahner believed that every human being is open to the presence of God simply by virtue of being human. In the universally human experiences of love and spiritual freedom, every human being encounters God as the "Holy Mystery" that forms the foundation of our lives as spiritual beings. God becomes present within our lives as Holy Mystery when, out of our free will, we choose to put aside violence or power-filled autonomy and respond to life out of love and forgiveness. Thus, in acts of compassion and generosity, in the struggle for justice, in the renunciation of revenge, in the befriending of the stranger, and in fidelity to love, God comes to be experienced as the unfathomable foundation of our lives. This experience of Mystery does not impose itself on us as an undeniable fact. The experience is easily denied or ignored or explained away. In addition, the experience of God as Mystery can never be fully analyzed or explained.

In contrast to Rahner, Barth's emphasis is on the gulf that separates God from sinful human beings. In Barth's view, human beings are radically cut off from contact with God by their own self-destructive pride and self-deluded vanity. Reflecting on our lives cannot lead us to God because we are so utterly lost within our own sinfulness. At best, our life experience can show us how helpless we are without the grace of God. God can be known only when God freely chooses to reveal himself to his sinful creature. And in fact God has revealed himself to human beings in the historical event that now is decisive for every human life: the death and resurrection of Jesus Christ.

Second, Karl Barth emphasized the fact that God is revealed only when and where he chooses to reveal himself. God is not experienced as an ineffable Holy Mystery that is implicit in every experience of love and freedom, regardless of what our religious beliefs might be. God is experienced as the word of judgment that exposes us as sinners even as it saves us from our vanity and foolishness. Thus, Rahner's understanding of revelation leads us to look for God everywhere; Barth's understanding of revelation calls us to reject the world and all our human philosophies and religions and to make a life-changing decision for Jesus Christ, the one and only Word of God. Thus, for Rahner, to the extent that religions represent the universal human quest to express the Holy Mystery in love and freedom, Christians should expect to find in non-Christian religions the same saving grace of Jesus Christ they find in their own religion. For Barth, religions are ingenious attempts to hide from God and avoid making a decision for Christ.

Third, Rahner and Barth are in complete agreement when it comes to the necessity of Christ for salvation. The salvation of human beings is always the result of the grace of the one God revealed in Jesus Christ. Both exclusivists, like Barth, and inclusivists, like Rahner, are Christocentric: all salvation is in Christ Jesus, the unique Word of God and final revelation of the living God. Exclusivists and inclusivists disagree on how this grace is available to human beings. Inclusivists tend to be more comfortable with the "cosmic Christ." By rising from the dead, the historical individual Jesus of Nazareth is now present throughout creation as cosmic Lord and savior. Exclusivists tend to prefer the historical Jesus, the Word of God who entered into history at a particular time and place, preached a particular gospel, and founded a particular community, the church, to carry on his work. Jesus was not born in India or China. The kingdom he proclaimed is the fulfillment of the hope of Israel, not Benaras or Shao-lin. The gospel of Jesus Christ must be brought to India and China. It cannot be discovered, hidden, within Hinduism or Buddhism.

The Anonymous Christian: Responsible to the Tradition?

I have said that any adequate theology of religions must be responsible to the faith of Christians and at the same time must assist Christian believers in dealing creatively with religious diversity. If this standard applies to exclusivist theologians like Barth, it must also apply to inclusivists like Karl Rahner. How does inclusivism measure up?

Rahner's theology of the anonymous Christian is not without precedents in Christian history. Many passages in the Bible speak of God's will to save all human beings.[24] In addition, there is a long tradition within Christianity of affirming that God's grace extends beyond the boundaries of the church community. In the second century, Justin Martyr argued that non-Christians, who live according to the truth, are

Christians at least implicitly.[25] In the Middle Ages, theologians such as Aquinas noted that there was a "baptism by desire" in which non-Christians could be saved by the grace of God without being baptized formally as Christians. In a famous case in 1952 involving Leonard Feeney, an American Jesuit, the Vatican rejected the view that outside the church there was no grace.[26] Nevertheless, protests against Rahner's theology of the anonymous Christian have been vociferous, and these voices have not gone away.[27]

Is the theology of the anonymous Christian responsible to the demands of the Christian tradition? Many of Rahner's critics argued that it is not an adequate response to religious diversity in this respect. If non-Christians are, or at least can be, "Christians without the name," then has Rahner not extended the boundaries of the church so far beyond the visible community of Christian believers that the notion of the "church" has become meaningless?

Hans Küng, one of Rahner's most strident critics, argued that if non-Christians are actually "Christians without the name," then membership in the church has been expanded to include everyone of generic good will.[28] If Muslims are Christians, only anonymously, then are atheists also to be included in the fold? Küng castigated Rahner's approach as merely a "theological trick" to sweep everyone into the church via the back door. There is a costly price to pay for this move, argued Küng. When the church becomes equivalent to almost everyone in the world, then what is to be said of the demanding message of the gospel to renounce all and become a disciple of Jesus Christ? This suggests a second problem for the theology of the anonymous Christian in relation to the Christian tradition.

Henri de Lubac, one of Rahner's best critics, protested that the theology of the anonymous Christian makes formal conversion to Christianity unnecessary. This is true in several ways. First, if Jains and Daoists can be saved by being good Jains and Daoists, is there anything unique and necessary about the Christian community? De Lubac reminds us that the gospel is a radical call to set aside our nets at the Sea of Galilee and follow Christ in a life of discipleship. Second, if there are several ways to salvation, is there anything unique about Jesus Christ as the historical incarnation of God within the world? Christianity teaches that in Jesus of Nazareth the Second Person of the Holy Trinity has come into the world as a specific human being. If so, does this not make Jesus profoundly different from Siddhartha Gautama, the historical Buddha? De Lubac argues that Christian belief in the divinity of Jesus separates Christianity from the other religions. Third, to claim that there are several ways to salvation would mean that our adherence to the truth ultimately separates us from one another. The human religious quest causes us to be dispersed into divergent paths that teach different doctrines. In effect, Rahner's theology of the anonymous Christian makes the non-Christian religions into rival churches.[29] But even in the light of this problem, de Lubac still agrees with Rahner that saving grace can be found at work in the lives of non-Christian believers. Thus he suggests that we can properly speak of non-Christian believers as "anonymous Christians," but we should not speak of Hinduism, Buddhism, Daoism, and the other religious traditions as forms of "anonymous Christianity." Individual non-Christians are saved by the grace of Jesus Christ acting universally, but this grace is not available through non-Christian religious traditions as such.

The Anonymous Christian: Helpful for Today?

Does Rahner's program for an inclusivist theology of religions assist Christians in living creatively with the diversity of religions today? On this issue, two criticisms of Rahner demand our attention.

First, Rahner's theology of the anonymous Christian has been criticized for providing an excuse for Christians to ignore the challenge posed to their religion by religious diversity. In effect, these critics are claiming that Rahner's inclusivism absolves Christians from the need to learn about non-Christians and their religions. Of course, this was not Rahner's intent. An unhappy side-effect of Rahner's theology, however, is that it puts Christians into a position of claiming to know more about non-Christians than they know about themselves.

Let me give some examples. A Confucian may be talking about the basis of our moral duties to parents and society in terms of our compliance with the "will of Heaven" (*T'ien*). But since the Confucian is really an "anonymous Christian," Christians know in advance what the Confucian does not: the "will of Heaven" is really the guiding grace of the God revealed most fully in the life and death of Jesus Christ.

When a Muslim claims that Jesus was a prophet and not a divine savior, that Jesus did not die on the cross or rise from the dead, Christians know what the Muslim does not, namely, that the grace of Jesus Christ, the divine savior of the world, is at work in the heart of the Muslim's religion.

Rahner responded to this criticism by saying that Christians should not use the term *anonymous Christian* as a label for non-Christians.[30] Instead, his inclusivist theology should be thought of as a program for guiding Christians in their relations with their non-Christian neighbors. The idea that non-Christians are Christians "without the name" is not a demand that Buddhists and Daoists correct their foolish and ignorant ways. Neither did Rahner want to suggest that Christians somehow know more about their non-Christian neighbors than they know about themselves. Rather, Rahner wanted to get Christians to look on non-Christian religions with the greatest of respect and reverence and to remember that the Mystery of God is far more than Christians imagine.[31]

Rahner's intent is certainly praiseworthy, but the theology of the anonymous Christian is inadequate to the challenge facing Christians today. Rahner's inclusivist approach implies that Christians know the relationship between their religion and other religions irrespective of any concrete knowledge of those other religions. Since the lengthy and difficult matter of interreligious dialogue will eventually reveal the work of the Holy Spirit within the religious life of the Muslim or the Confucian, there is never any pressing necessity to learn about these religions. The theology of the anonymous Christian was never intended to distract Christians from learning about other religious believers, although sometimes this has been its practical effect. The point is that Rahner's inclusivism does not lead Christians to learn about other religions as a creative response to religious diversity today.

Second, to the extent that Rahner's inclusivist theology can serve as an excuse for not learning *about* our non-Christian neighbors, it also serves as an excuse for not learning *from* them. Neither is this unhappy side effect Rahner's intention, but it is a weakness in his approach which must be recognized. If we look deeply enough into the lives of our non-Christian neighbors, we will find there what we already know. Even if this expectation does not extinguish our curiosity about other religions, Rahner's theological program for dealing with religious diversity tends to highlight the similarities that Christianity shares with other religions. It also tends to blind us to the real, enduring differences, which distinguish non-Christian religions from Christianity. If we look into the lives of non-Christians and find there troubling, destabilizing differences that cannot easily be integrated into our own, Christian view of ourselves and the world, apparently this means that we have not looked deeply enough. Ultimately, in the lives of our non-Christian neighbors, we will find the same grace at work that we know about already as Christian believers. This means that non-Christians have nothing of real significance to teach Christians. Since there are no surprises in Rahner's program, there is no real learning from one another either. This problem must be counted a major weakness in the whole idea of an inclusivist theology of religions.[32]

*   *   *

Can exclusivism and inclusivism be counted adequate Christian responses to the intrusive fact of religious diversity today? Both models for a theology of religions have their supporters. Both models have their critics. Are these two views of the many religions adequate to the demands of the Christian tradition? Do they empower Christians to live creatively with the fact of religious diversity? Rahner's inclusivist theology is more in keeping with the Christian tradition than Barth's exclusivism. Neither Barth nor Rahner, however, provides Christians with a theological understanding of non-Christians and their religions that is adequate to the needs of Christian believers today.

More recently, a third option for an adequate theology of religions has come on the scene, the pluralist option. The controversy over the pluralist theology of religions has made the earlier debates between the exclusivists and inclusivists seem tame by comparison. In the chapter to follow, we begin a discussion of one of the foremost exponents of a pluralist theology of religions, John Hick.

NOTES

1. The first to suggest this threefold typology was Alan Race in his *Christians and Religious Pluralism: Patterns in the Christian Theology of Religions* (Maryknoll, N.Y.: Orbis Books, 1982).

2. Karl Barth, *Church Dogmatics* 1/2, ed. G. W Bromiley and T. F. Torrance (Edinburgh: T. & T. Clark, 1956), especially 297–325.

3. Ibid., 301.

4. Ibid., 308.

5. Ibid., 301.

6. Ibid., 299–302.

7. Ibid., 299–300.

8. Ibid., 314.

9. Ibid., 300.

10. Ibid., 299.

11. Ibid.

12. Ibid., 325ff.

13. Ibid., 326–27.

14. Shubert Ogden believes that this double standard constitutes a new form of evil, unprecedented in Christian thought. I disagree. Exclusivism's double standard actually reaches back to the early days of Christianity and its controversy with groups such as the Marcionites, the Manicheans and other Gnostics. In the first several centuries after Christ, the Manicheans, for example, argued that the world is fundamentally evil and salvation amounts to an escape from this evil. Therefore, the evil god who created the evil world is not at all the good God who rescues his chosen ones from the world. Implied in this view is the belief that the world tells us nothing about the God who redeems us. Those who happen to have been chosen by the redeemer God are saved. Those who do not know this redeemer God know only the evil god of creation and are damned. The church fathers, most prominently Irenaeus of Lyon, argued that the God of creation and the God of redemption are one. Thus, to know creation is to know the God who not only creates but also redeems. Does this anti-Gnostic tradition in Christianity suggest that non-Christians must have some implicit knowledge of the God of Jesus Christ simply by virtue of their human experience of the world? If that is the case, then, contrary to Barth, no human being can be said to be utterly separated from God. For Ogden's treatment of exclusivism, see *Is There One True Religion or Are There Many?* (Dallas: Southern Methodist University Press, 1992), 40–48.

15. D. Niles, "Karl Barth—A Personal Memory," *South East Asian*

Journal of Theology 11 (1969): 10–11. See also Gavin D'Costa, *Theology and Religious Pluralism: The Challenge of Other Religions* (Oxford: Basil Blackwell, 1986), 54.

16. For discussions of the relationship between Pure Land Buddhism and Christianity, see the following: Gerhard Schepers, "Shinran's View of the Human Predicament and the Christian Concept of Sin," *Japanese Religions 15* (July 1988): 1–17; Charles T. Waldrop, "Karl Barth and Pure Land Buddhism," *Journal of Ecumenical Studies* 24 (Fall 1987): 574–97; Masatoshi Doi, "Dynamics of Faith: A Dialogical Study of Pure Land Buddhism and Evangelical Christianity," *Japanese Religions* 11, nos. 2–3 (Summer 1980): 56–73; Paul D. Ingram, "Shinran Shonin and Martin Luther: A Soteriological Comparison," *Journal of the American Academy of Religion* 39 (December 1971): 430–47; Hajime Nakamura, "Pure Land Buddhism and Western Christianity Compared: A Quest for the Common Roots of Their Universality," *International Journal for Philosophy of Religion* 1 (Summer 1970): 77–96.

17. Barth, *Church Dogmatics,* 1/2, 343. Note Barth's oblique reference to Acts 4:12.

18. *The Documents of Vatican II,* ed. Walter Abbott, S.J. (New York: America Press, 1966), 662.

19. Karl Rahner, "Christianity and the Non-Christian Religions," in *Theological Investigations* V (Baltimore, Md.: Helicon Press, 1966), 115–34.

20. Ibid., 121.

21. More recently, the possibility that salvation in Christ might be seen not only in the lines of individual non-Christians but in non-Christian religions themselves has been raised by John Paul II in several official statements. For a discussion of papal teachings on this matter, see Francis Sullivan, *Salvation Outside the Church?* (Mahwah, N.J.: Paulist Press, 1992). Along with John Paul II, Jacques Dupuis, a Catholic theologian with many years of experience learning in India, has taken up Rahner's notion that non-Christian religions as such can be ways of salvation in Christ in a book that is the best contemporary statement of the inclusivist position. See Jacques Dupuis, *Jesus Christ at the Encounter of World Religions,* trans. Robert R. Barr (Maryknoll, N.Y.: Orbis Books, 1991).

22. Rahner "Christianity and the Non-Christian Religions," 131.

23. Ibid., 133.

24. For example, in the Acts of the Apostles see Acts 10:34–35 and Acts 17:23–28. Among Paul's epistles see Phil 4:8, and Rom 2:12–16. In the Pastoral Letters, see 1 Tm 2:4 and 4:10.

25. Justin Martyr *Apologia* 1.46. Justin held that as Abraham had an

implicit knowledge of the Word of God (the eternal *Logos Spermatikos*), so also did non-Christians like Plato. Thus, one may come to the explicit revelation of God in the Christian church by following the implicit revelation in non-Christian wisdom such as Platonic philosophy.

26. For a careful treatment of the Leonard Feeney case, see Sullivan, *Salvation Outside the Church?*

27. Rahner replied to his critics in a series of articles on the subject of an inclusivist theology of religions. See Karl Rahner "Observations on the Problem of the 'Anonymous Christian,'" in *Theological Investigations* XIV (New York: The Seabury Press, 1976), 280; idem, "Anonymous and Explicit Faith," in *Theological Investigations* XVI (New York: Crossroad, 1979) 52–59; idem, "The One Christ and the Universality of Salvation," in ibid., 199–201.

28. Hans Küng, *On Being a Christian* (Garden City, N.Y.: Doubleday, 1976), 97–99.

29. Henri de Lubac, S.J., *Paradox et Mystère de l'Eglise* (Paris: Editions du Cerf, 1967), 153–56.

30. Rahner, "Observations on the Problem of the 'Anonymous Christian,'" 280.

31. Karl Rahner, "Atheism and Implicit Christianity," in *Theological Investigations* IX (New York: Herder and Herder, 1972), 45–64.

32. The view that Rahner's theology of the anonymous Christian can serve as an adequate basis for entering into interreligious dialogue has an articulate supporter in Maurice Boutin. For his defense of Rahner, see Maurice Boutin, "Anonymous Christianity: A Paradigm for Interreligious Encounter?" *Journal of Ecumenical Studies* 20, no. 4 (Fall 1983): 602–29.

Chapter 2

JOHN HICK'S COPERNICAN REVOLUTION

In a famous scene of the *Bhagavad Gita*, one of the most often cited of the Hindu scriptures, the charioteer Krishna, who is an *avatar,* or worldly manifestation of the supreme deity, Vishnu, proclaims:

> Howsoever men may approach me, even so do I accept them; for,
> on all sides, whatever path they may choose is mine.

Inspired at least in part by these comforting words from the Hindu scriptures, John Hick has started what he hopes will be a lasting revolution in our thinking about the diversity of religions in the world.

John Hick is to be admired for being a thinker and a religious believer who has had the courage, to say nothing of the humility, to change his mind a great deal about some very important matters. His religious quest led him first to a strongly evangelical brand of Christianity that rightly could be called fundamentalist. His intellectual honesty, however, would not allow him to persist in his exclusivist beliefs. Not the least of the challenges he faced as a Presbyterian pastor in Birmingham, England, was the diversity of religious traditions he encountered working among Hindus, Muslims, Sikhs, and Jews. This experience led him to begin a long process of working out a suitable theory to account for the diversity of religious paths in the world today.[1]

37

A Copernican Revolution

John Hick began his revolution in 1973 with the publication of his first book to deal explicitly with the problem of religious diversity, *God and the Universe of Faiths*.[2] Christians must undergo what Hick called a "Copernican revolution" in their understanding of their faith in relation to the vast diversity of religious traditions in the world. In the fifteenth century, Copernicus overturned the Ptolemaic view of the universe by placing the sun at the center and designating the earth as the third planet out from the sun. In one simple stroke, this Polish priest abandoned centuries of belief about the stability of the earth at the center of the universe, to say nothing of the authority of Aristotle and the Bible. Hick's revolution, however, has to do not with the universe of planets but rather with the universe of religions. As Copernicus argued for a heliocentric model of the solar system, where the sun replaces the earth as the center of all, Hick argued for a "theocentric" theology of religions, where God alone and not Christ or the Christian church is given pride of place at the center of things.

Europeans presumed for centuries that the earth was the center of the solar system. Careful observation of the planets as they make their way through the heavens against the background of the fixed stars, however, called Ptolemy's view of things into question. To protect Ptolemy's time-honored model of the universe, medieval astronomers in Europe were required to add an elaborate and implausible system of epicycles to the orbits of the planets.

Christian exclusivism, Hick maintained, was the theological equivalent to Ptolemy's geocentric model of the solar system. In keeping with this comparison, inclusivist theologies of religions are like the epicycles used to keep the earth safely in the center of the solar system and protect Ptolemy's model. For example, Rahner's argument that non-Christians be considered "anonymous Christians" amounts to nothing more than a cumbersome and implausible addition to the traditional Christian teaching regarding the necessity of Christ for salvation. Inclusivist theologies were made necessary in order to preserve traditional Christian teaching about Jesus Christ as the one and only savior of the world after it became impossible for Christians to ignore the reality of non-Christian religions. Inclusivist theologies, to use another metaphor, had not yet crossed the theological Rubicon into territory where the plurality of religions was really taken seriously. Hick thinks that these theologies are implicitly exclusivist in their outlook: salvation can only be in the name of Jesus Christ. The medieval notion of baptism by desire, like Karl Rahner's theology of the "anonymous Christian," is a contrivance that succeeds only in avoiding the inevitable. In a world of vast religious diversity, Christianity's claim to be the only true religion is hopelessly naive. Given the reality of religious diversity today, Christians will have to abandon their traditional teaching about the necessity of faith in Jesus Christ for salvation.

Hick wants Christianity to undergo a revolution in its thinking about the many religions that human beings embrace in this world. This revolution removes Christianity from the center of the universe of faiths and replaces it, at least in Hick's early work, with the utterly transcendent God who lies beyond all religious paths.

> And we have to realize that the universe of faiths centers upon
> *God*, and not upon Christianity or upon any other religion. He is
> the sun, the originative source of life and light, whom all the reli-
> gions reflect in their own different ways.[3]

Since every religion reflects the light of the same divine sun, each religion points in its own way to this transcendent God. Thus, in every religion there lies at least the possibility for a believer to have a genuine encounter with the divine. The religions of the world must be seen as hugely complex responses to the mysterious presence that lies at the foundation of them all. The innumerable symbols, doctrines, ethical rules, and rituals that are the legacy of the world's religious traditions inspire human beings because they all reflect the one divine light that shines through the universe of the many faiths.

Can it be true that Hindus and Buddhists, Muslims and Daoists, Jews and Jains, Christians and Confucians all worship the same God? Hick finds support for his theocentric model in the fact that all religions claim, to one degree or another, the inadequacy of words for conveying the truth of their teachings. In Hinduism, for example, the Upanishads insist that words break down before the infinity of Brahman. In the opening passage of the *Dao-de-Jing*, we are warned that the Dao that can be expressed in words is not the eternal Dao. Theravada Buddhists note that Nirvana utterly eludes every concept we might try to attribute to it. Mahayana Buddhists claim the same thing about the *Dharmakaya* and the Buddha Nature. Christians, of course, generally fall right into line on this score, starting with Paul's peace that surpasses all understanding and continuing through the silence of the mystics before the incomprehensible mystery of God.

From statements such as these, which punctuate the scriptures and theologies of the many religions of the world, Hick reaches his daring and controversial conclusion. The fact that there are differences that distinguish religions from one another does not necessarily imply that the truth proclaimed by one religious tradition excludes the truth of another religion. Differing religious truths can all be complementary.

The complementarity of religious truths, of course, is not always easy to see. Shiva, India's erotic ascetic, would not seem to have very much in common with Allah on the surface of things. Likewise Yahweh, speaking to Moses atop Mount Sinai, does not seem at all equivalent to T'ien ("Heaven") extolled by Confucians. But Hick is not claiming that all these religious symbols are the same. Hick wants us to see Shiva, Allah, Yahweh, and T'ien as different reflections of a single transcendent divine reality that lies infinitely beyond them all. The one mysterious divinity is manifest in remarkably different ways.

All religions must begin to understand themselves *theo*-centrically. All religious doctrines, concepts, and symbols point beyond themselves to the incomprehensible and inexpressible mystery of the divine itself. Therefore, contrary to exclusivist and inclusivist views, no religion can claim to occupy the center of the universe of faiths. No religion can claim to be superior to another. This goes for Christianity too. Each religion offers a different path for encountering the same mysterious God lying transcendently beyond them all. Christ is one path, but there are other names.

The Myth of God Incarnate

Hick's call for a Copernican revolution in our understanding of religious diversity inaugurated a debate that has continued to the present. In defending his views against his critics, Hick has argued that his pluralistic theology of religions, based on a move to theocentrism, is required by Christian faith itself. Hick reminds his critics that Christianity has taught from the beginning that God's will to save every human being is universal. No one, no matter what his or her religion might be, is excluded in principle from the divine offer of salvation. In this respect, Hick has no quarrel with Christianity's claim about the universality of God's will to save. But this teaching, please note, is only one of the two Christian affirmations that every theology of religions must address. The other affirmation has to do with the uniqueness of Jesus. How does Jesus Christ figure into Hick's pluralistic theology of religions?

As Christians have extolled the infinite mercy of God and God's universal will to save, Christians have also maintained the necessity of faith in Christ for salvation. Jesus of Nazareth, Christians have traditionally held, is the one and only incarnation of the living God within human history, the final revelation, the Lord of all history. For this reason, all salvation must be through faith in Jesus Christ, at least implicitly. The theocentric model of the universe of faiths does not seem to be compatible with this time-honored Christian teaching. John Hick faces this problem head-on.

In 1977, Hick shepherded into print a collection of essays by various authors entitled *The Myth of God Incarnate*. This volume included an essay of his own entitled "Jesus and the World Religions."[4] In this essay, Hick developed an interpretation of Jesus Christ that did little to quell the flames of controversy surrounding his pluralistic theology of religions. The theocentric model of religions, in Hick's view, does require Christians to abandon their belief in the absolute necessity of faith in Jesus Christ for salvation. Although this is the case, Hick also argued that his Copernican revolution does not require Christians to jettison their belief in the uniqueness of Jesus as God become incarnate within history as a particular human being.

Christianity's doctrine of the incarnation, a teaching that did not take its final form until some four hundred years after the birth of Jesus, holds that Jesus of Nazareth was at once fully human and fully divine. In Hick's view, this teaching should not be taken as a literal fact. Taking the incarnation as a literal fact leads inevitably to an exclusivist mentality, where those who have accepted Jesus as Lord are saved and the vast majority of human beings who have ever lived are damned. The belief that Jesus was fully human and at the same time fully divine must be understood a kind of "myth."

In calling the incarnation a "myth," however, Hick does not mean to suggest that Christians should abandon their belief in Jesus as a savior. Belief in the divinity of Jesus is not merely a mistake and an illusion. The doctrine of the incarnation is a poetic way of expressing a truth that cannot be stated directly and should not be taken literally. For most scholars interested in religion (including theologians), "myth" means a model or paradigm for understanding in a nonliteral fashion realities that are considerably more complex. Much like the language of poetry, myths are true, but not literally true. In fact, to take a myth literally is seriously to misunderstand it.

An obvious example of a myth being used to express a religious truth is the account of the seven days of creation in the first chapter of Genesis. Most Christians today believe that this story expresses an important truth about the sovereignty of God as transcendent Lord over all creation. But to interpret this biblical passage to mean that the heavens and the earth were literally created in seven calendar days would be a serious misreading of the story. Only by reading the story of creation as a myth does its real meaning become apparent.

Is the incarnation a "myth" in this sense of the word? In defense of his controversial position, Hick argues that Christians should think of the incarnation as a model or paradigm for affirming the saving power of God at work in their lives. Christians talk about this saving power of God by proclaiming that "Jesus Christ is Lord." In Jesus Christ, at once the new Adam and the Second Person of the Holy Trinity, God and the human race have become perfectly reconciled to one another once again. The incarnation, then, is a way of imagining what is beyond all imagining: the infinitely transcendent God touching the lives of each and every human being.

Hick, however, wants Christians to recognize that the incarnation is not the only way God's salvation can be imagined. In fact, Hick claims that the incarnation, as this doctrine was developed in the first several centuries of the Christian church, should be seen as merely a Greco-Roman way of affirming the saving power of God. As a way of conceptualizing our salvation, the incarnation is not very universal at all. In India, for example, some Hindus sing the praises of Krishna, the earthly appearance (*avatar*) of the transcendent deity Vishnu. Other Hindus think of salvation in terms of the cultivation of the true self (*atman*) through meditation. Muslims talk of submission to the will of Allah as revealed in the Qur'an and find Christianity's claim that Jesus was divine blasphemous. In China, Daoists hope to achieve immortality through harmony with the natural and spontaneous arising of the Dao. All of these religious beliefs are models for talking about what is completely beyond words, what Hick means by "myth."

The incarnation is merely one of several ways available to human beings for thinking about how God saves us. In addition, Hick thinks this doctrine is not particularly well suited to the needs of Christians trying to negotiate the modern world and its increased awareness of religious diversity.[5] To the extent that the doctrine makes claims about a real historical person, Jesus of Nazareth, Hick believes that the incarnation can easily be understood in a dangerously literal way. The Christian churches have been slow to accept, to the extent that they have accepted at all, the criticism that secular historians have made of this doctrine. Like Siddhartha Gautama, the historical Buddha, Jesus was exalted by his followers into divinity only years after his death.[6] Both of these promotions are the result of human longing for a personal savior. Christians are not the only religious believers who have divinized their founders and then taken it as a literal fact. This weakness in other religions, according to Hick, does not excuse Christians from recognizing the mythic character of their own claim that Jesus is divine.

Hick was fully aware that his mythological view of the incarnation would ruffle quite a few Christian feathers and, in his controversial essay, he was ready with a reply to at least one of their objections. Christianity has traditionally claimed that Jesus rose from the dead. Many Christians, although not all, take this as proof of his divinity. If Jesus rose from the dead, he must be divine and the incarnation is a historical fact, not merely a myth. To this objection Hick points out that in the New Testament the resurrection is not seen as a proof that Jesus was truly God. The resurrection itself is an interpretation of the fate of Jesus after his death. The New Testament accounts of the resurrection are careful to note that no one was an eyewitness to what happened to Jesus after his death. Sometime after Jesus' death, the disciples of Jesus came to believe that their sins were forgiven and that they had been given a mission to spread the good news of God's salvation through Christ to the ends of the earth. They symbolized this dramatic transformation of their lives by saying that Jesus was "risen" from the dead. Therefore, the resurrection, like the incarnation, is not to be taken literally. Jesus' rising from the dead is a mythological way for Christians to profess their faith in the saving power of Jesus.[7]

If these considerations are noted, Hick concludes, the doctrine of the incarnation need not stand as a barrier to Christians in embracing a theocentric theology of religions. Jesus' divinity is not to be taken as a literal historical fact. The notion of an incarnation can be a fitting way for some religious people (Christians) to express their experience of being saved by a divine power that is at work in all the religions. This myth, however, is by no means the only way.[8] When taken literally, the myth of the incarnation becomes downright toxic. To the extent that the incarnation is taken literally, Christians are led to an exclusivist or inclusivist understanding of non-Christians and their religions. Understanding the incarnation as a myth frees Christians to adopt a theocentric understanding of religions. All the great religions make available to their believers the same salvation that Christians experience in Christ because all of these religions are responses to the one mysterious God that transcends them all. Faith in Jesus Christ is not the only way to talk about or "model" this salvation, although it is an acceptable way for Christians to talk about it, provided this "talk" is not taken literally.

The World Is Religiously Ambiguous

Hick's theocentric view of religions carries with it a tangled knot of complications. Thus far, we have only looked at the problem the theocentric model posed for the traditional Christian understanding of the uniqueness of Jesus and the necessity of faith in Christ for salvation. Another problem that Hick had to solve in much greater depth has to do with how we can know that there is one divine reality behind all the great religions of the world. How can this be when what religious people say, at least on the surface, seems so different, even contradictory? If all the religions reflect one divine mystery that lies beyond them all, what does it mean to say that a Buddhist and a Muslim have different experiences of the same transcendent reality? Hick realized that he needed to clarify what he meant by a "religious experience."

To defend his pluralist model, John Hick must explain how religious believers who say very different things about important matters such as the human predicament, the character of God, and life after death are in fact all talking about the same transcendent reality. In this regard, Hick turned to the philosophy of Immanuel Kant (1724–1804).[9] Kant was a German philosopher whose thought, perhaps more than that of any other, can be associated with the European Enlightenment and the modern scientific worldview that came out of it.

As a philosopher working in the midst of the scientific revolution, more than anything else Kant wanted to understand what it means to know. At the center of Kant's philosophy is his conviction that all human knowledge is limited. Our experience of the world is drastically constrained by the way our mind factors raw sense data into preset categories such as shape, color, and quantity. Because of this inescapable fact, Kant was led to make his famous distinction between a thing as it is in itself (the *noumenon*) and a thing as it is experienced by the human mind (the *phenomenon*).

Philosophers have been building on Kant's basic ideas for some time. Today many would agree that all knowledge is to some degree subjective in the sense that our experience of the world is shaped by the language we speak, our cultural traditions, and our personal presuppositions. In knowing the world around it, the mind is not merely a passive receiver of objective facts. Each mind selects sense data and organizes it into a coherent interpretation of experience. Building on Kant, Hick emphasizes the point that we "make sense" out of the chaotic whirlwind of the senses by using the concepts, metaphors, and presuppositions that make up the "common sense" of our culture.

Examples of what Hick is getting at are bountiful. The Eskimo language has multiple words for snow. This fact would suggest that they look on snowstorms differently than a Bedouin wandering in Saudi Arabia's Empty Quarter who has never encountered slush, let alone corncob or Colorado powder. Modern Chinese people look on comets differently than their medieval counterparts because their presuppositions about celestial events are different. If a tribal group presumes that illness is caused by the casting of spells and has no concept of bacterial infection, we should expect them to look for a sorcerer when one of their number suddenly falls ill. The impressions a Russian takes home from a performance of *Boris Gudonov* will be different from those of someone who grew up with the Beijing Opera because their views about drama and music as well as their languages are different.[10]

Hick used Kant's distinction between reality as it is in itself and reality as it is known by human beings to explain his notion of religious experience. The divine mystery always remains transcendent and is never known in itself. The God at the center of the universe of faiths is always known imperfectly—"through a glass darkly," as the apostle Paul says. Human beings experience the divine in terms of their own cultural background and expectations. For this reason, "to experience" always means "to experience as," or "to interpret." The great religions of the world are hugely complex tools for making religious sense out of life. Religious diversity results from the simple fact that different human beings can make sense out of the one divine mystery in a number of different ways.[11]

Here again, examples are bountiful. Some religions provide their adherents with complex legal systems. In Judaism, the *Torah* is an encompassing interpretation of the meaning of life in the face of the ultimate mystery of God. The same is true of Islam's *Sharia*, even though neither the spirit nor the letter of Qur'anic Law is the same as in the Mosaic Law. Christians look on the reality of suffering and death in terms of hope in God because the death and resurrection of Jesus Christ are such a powerful symbol in their lives. Buddhists interpret this same reality by reflecting on the *parinirvana* of the Buddha. In India, a Muslim and a Hindu may both look upon a man blind from birth but interpret this fact in significantly different ways.

The world, therefore, is "religiously ambiguous"[12] according to Hick. Acting in good faith, human beings can interpret the religious meaning of life in a variety of different ways. Since "the true character of the universe does not force itself on us,"[13] more than one religious interpretation of life can be true. The mystery of God at the center of the universe of faiths may be expressed with Shiva's Dance or with the notion of Divine Providence, the interplay of *yin-yang*, or numeric symbolism within the Kabbalah. Given this ambiguity, the plurality of religious claims about the divine should come as no surprise. Religions are culturally based systems of ideas, symbols, and rituals that enable us to experience the world in certain ways and not in others. No religious claim is based on an irrefutably "objective" observation of the world. Religious doctrines are always interpretations of a transcendent divine reality that can be interpreted in more than one way.

In his later writings, Hick offers a number of analogies to elucidate what he means when he says that the world is religiously ambiguous. Physicists have long puzzled over the nature of light. Some experiments can be performed which show that light is a particle. Other experiments can be performed which show that light must be a wave. Well, is it a particle or a wave? The reality lies beyond these conflicting models. Neither the wave theory nor the particle theory is wrong. Moreover, despite the apparent contradiction, neither of the two interpretations can exclude the other. Hick also refers to map making. Since the surface of a sphere cannot be depicted on a two dimensional surface without some distortion, cartographers interested in constructing maps of the entire world have worked out various compromises to get around this dilemma. Mercator's famous solution to the problem is successful but is not the only possibility for mapping the whole globe. As with the nature of light in physics, one solution being correct does not imply that other solutions are incorrect. One type of map may be more useful for a particular purpose than for other purposes. Mercator projections, for example, are not particularly useful for Arctic travelers.

Religions are like models in physics or maps in geography. They offer human beings interpretations of the religious meaning of life: models of human existence, maps of the real. All religions, according to Hick, are but poor approximations of the truth. Like the two possibilities for understanding light in physics, one religious interpretation of life does not necessarily invalidate another interpretation, even a contradictory interpretation. Like the multitude of ways cartographers can project the globe onto a flat piece of paper, some interpretations of life are more useful than others in certain situations.[14]

From Theocentrism to Reality-Centeredness

Hick's pluralist theology of religions, with its theocentric revolution, its mythological understanding of the divinity of Jesus, and its Kantian understanding of religious experience, lit a fire under many theologians. Voices for and against Hick's approach to religious diversity began to be heard in abundance. In 1985, Hick published *Problems of Religious Pluralism*, another important contribution to the pluralism debate, which responded to his critics by tackling head-on some of the more intractable problems associated with his pluralist theology.[15] Among other reasons, this work is significant in that it marks a move away from his theocentric model of religions to what he today calls "reality-centeredness."

In his earlier work, Hick argued that all religions were in fact responses to the one transcendent "God" or "divine reality," which lies beyond them all. In *Problems of Religious Pluralism*, Hick amended this view by saying that the great religions, in different ways, put their adherents in touch with the "Real" as it is in itself. Salvation, which is available in all the great religious traditions, entails a movement from self-centeredness to reality-centeredness.[16] Each of the great religions offers human beings a way of freeing themselves from the prison of their own ego for a life lived in unity with reality itself, however this unity may be interpreted within the religious traditions themselves.

In moving to reality-centeredness, Hick has drastically expanded the meaning of the term *salvation*. To the extent that Christians understand salvation as the forgiveness of our sins and being reconciled with God by the atoning death of Jesus, then obviously all salvation is available only through the grace of Jesus Christ. But Hick believes salvation should be defined more psychologically as a transformation of the ego. All religions offer their believers paths that lead to the liberation of the self from greed, cruelty, obsession, and fear. We are "saved" when we move from being centered on the ego to being centered on reality itself.

Hick's move from theo-centricity to reality-centeredness was motivated by his recognition that not all religions are particularly interested in the divine. Theravada Buddhism, for example, looks on the idea of faith in a creator God as an entanglement that creates more suffering. T'ien, the "Heaven" extolled by the Confucians, displays no personal characteristics, with the exception of having a will. The Dao cannot be characterized as a personal divinity in any sense. In Japan, Rinzai Zen teachers advise their students to kill the Buddha if they should meet the Buddha. To Hick, terms such as *the Real* or *Ultimate Reality* are better than words such as *God* or *the divine* because they are more inclusive of both the personal and impersonal conceptions of the absolute.

Are All Religions Really the Same?

Another problem faced squarely by Hick in *Problems of Religious Pluralism* has to do with the meaning of the many differences that distinguish religions from one another. Are all religions really the same at heart? A Jew begging God's help at the Wailing Wall, to all appearances at least, does not seem to be doing the same thing as a Daoist priest using the *I Jing* to divine the future. A Bengali mother placing a garland of marigolds before a statue of Krishna seems far removed from a Muslim reciting the *Shahada* ("There is no God but God and Muhammad is His Prophet"). However, Hick observes that all the great religious traditions are in agreement on at least one point that for him is singularly important: there is a higher reality that is beyond all language and utterly defeats our ability to conceptualize; and, furthermore, enlightenment or salvation consists in conforming our lives to this higher reality.[17]

To secure his point, Hick marshals examples from several religious traditions. Christians are quite accustomed to speaking of the *deus absconditus* (i.e., the inconceivable divine mystery, unknown to human beings) and the *deus revelatus* (God as disclosed to human beings). Hindu pundits distinguish *niguna brahman* (Ultimate Reality without qualities whatsoever) and *saguna brahman* (Ultimate Reality with qualities).[18]

Human responses to the Real generally can be fitted into one of two basic types. Sometimes the Real is interpreted theistically as a person; sometimes it is interpreted nontheistically as an impersonal quality or principle. Yahweh, Allah, the Father, Son, and Holy Spirit, Shiva, Vishnu, and Amaterasu, to name only some of the more obvious candidates, are examples of the former. Brahman, the Dao, Emptiness, Dharmakaya, and the Buddha Nature are examples of the latter. In keeping with his conviction that the world is religiously ambiguous, Hick does not believe that the Real must be interpreted either as a personal deity or as an impersonal metaphysical absolute. Ultimate Reality is such that it can be seen either as a person or as an impersonal principle. Yahweh and Brahman, Allah and the Dao are different interpretations of the same ultimately unknowable absolute.[19]

In this regard, Hick fumes at his critics for claiming that he is suggesting that religions do not really make conflicting claims about human beings, the world, and the Real.[20] Christians believe that Jesus died on the cross. Muslims believe that he only appeared to die. Hindu belief in reincarnation must be starkly contrasted with Christianity's doctrine of the resurrection of the body. The purpose of a pluralistic theology of religions, Hick argues, is not to homogenize the religions of the world into one. Even though all salvation entails moving from ego-centeredness to reality-centeredness, the various religions differ from one another in the way they conceive, symbolize, and pursue this salvation. Hick believes that the pluralist model allows us to acknowledge that the differences separating religions are real without forcing religious believers into either exclusivism or inclusivism. Understood correctly, religious differences complement one another. When Buddhists talk about Nirvana as "the further shore," they are trying to interpret the same Ultimate Reality that Christians name God. Since both God and Nirvana lead human beings to abandon ego-centered living and take up reality-centered living, Christians and Buddhists can differ peacefully. Since all the great religious traditions empower human beings to undergo the same transformation from egocentricity to reality-centeredness, the differences that distinguish religions can be acknowledged as real but inconsequential to salvation.[21]

The Pluralistic Hypothesis

In 1989, Hick published *An Interpretation of Religion*, a work that remains his most comprehensive statement on the diversity of religions.[22] In this work, all the basic elements of Hick's program for a pluralistic model of religions are in place: salvation as reality-centeredness, the Kantian distinction between the Real in itself and the Real as it is known by human beings, the religious ambiguity of the universe, and, in addition, a final element to which we will now turn.

Hick maintains that "the great...faiths constitute different ways of experiencing, conceiving and living in relation to an ultimate divine Reality which transcends all our varied visions of it."[23] Religions involve different human conceptualizations of the Real and thus differing human experiences of the Real. The great religious traditions are thus differing responses to one and the same ultimate reality that transcends them all. Hick has maintained this view, more or less, since 1973. What is new, however, is that now John Hick claims that this statement should be taken only as a hypothesis.

Why is such a hypothesis necessary? Even a cursory glance at the world's religious phenomena confronts us with literally millions of gods. Do all these gods exist? This cursory glance will also turn up a library full of nonpersonal concepts of the ultimate. If the Real is the Buddha Nature or Brahman or the Dao, how can it be a personal deity? Modern critics of religious belief look on all these differing views of the ultimate as proof that all religions are wrong. Not a few religious believers have responded to this same whirlwind of religious phenomena by declaring dogmatically that their religion is true and all the others are false or partially in error or merely inferior versions of the real truth, which is readily available only in their own religion. But when believers defend their own religion against the arguments of the skeptics, it is increasingly difficult to say, "My religion is true and all the others are illusions." Very often an argument in defense of the truth of one religious doctrine also can be used to defend the doctrines of another religious tradition.[24] Taking pluralism seriously is unavoidable for religious believers today.

Having criticized the skeptical view that all religions are to be rejected as illusory and the dogmatic view that all religions are wrong to one degree or another with the exception of my own, Hick offers a third possibility: the pluralistic hypothesis. In order to live tolerantly in a world of vast religious diversity, believers ought to adopt as a working presupposition the belief that all religions should be taken to be different responses to the same ultimate reality. This statement is not an objective fact. Hick does not suggest that this view is an irrefutable conclusion based on an objective look at the world. Religious believers should adopt this view as a hypothesis that enables them to live peacefully with the diversity of faiths in the world. Without this hypothesis, believers are left with either skepticism or dogmatism in facing the universe of faiths.[25]

In what sense should Hick's pluralist model of religions be taken only as a hypothesis? To develop his point, Hick turns again to the philosopher Immanuel Kant. In Hick's interpretation of Kant's philosophy, God is not so much a reality present to human beings in their religious experience as a concept made necessary by the demands of morality. In order to make logical sense out of our personal sense of moral duty, the mind is required to postulate the existence of a highest good (the *summum bonum*). As the highest good, God is a necessary postulate of our moral reasoning. Without belief in God, at least theoretically, our moral lives cannot make sense. Somewhat analogously to Kant's understanding of God, Hick argues that we need to think of "the Real" as a postulate or hypothesis necessary for making sense of our pluralistic religious situation. Without postulating the Real as the transcendent source of all our diverse religious experiences, we are left with either skepticism or dogmatic absolutism. For Kant, God is a concept, not an experience. Similarly for Hick, the Real in itself is a concept, not an experience. What is experienced by human beings are all the phenomenal manifestations of the Real: the Holy Trinity and Allah, Brahman and the Dharmakaya, Vishnu and Ahura Mazuda.[26] Faced with the multitude of religious expressions, the concept of the "Real" needs to be adopted as a hypothesis. Without this hypothesis, skepticism or dogmatic absolutism are the only alternatives.

*   *   *

I have emphasized two criteria for evaluating the adequacy of a theology of religions. The first of the two is responsibility to the tradition. Any theology of religions must be accountable to the demands of the Christian tradition. The second of the two criteria is as important as the first. An adequate theology of religions must empower Christians to respond creatively to the challenge and opportunity posed by religious diversity today. For many Christians following the debate over pluralism,

John Hick's reality-centered model of religions sets off alarm bells re-garding the first of the two criteria. I agree. I also think Hick's pluralism fails to meet the demands of the second criterion. Before this issue can be addressed, we need to know more about the pluralist debate. Hick's approach to religious diversity is philosophical. He uses Kant's distinc-tion between reality as it is in itself and as it is known by human beings. This approach by no means is the only possible candidate for a pluralis-tic theology of religions. Other voices calling for a pluralistic theology are concerned more with the role Christianity and the other religions play in the struggle for justice by the poor. In the following chapter we will look at this alternative way of moving beyond exclusivism and in-clusivism.

NOTES

1. For Hick's own account of his "spiritual pilgrimage," see *God Has Many Names: Britain's New Religious Pluralism* (London: Macmillan, 1980), 1–9.

2. John Hick, *God and the Universe of Faiths* (New York: St. Martin's Press, 1973).

3. Hick, *God Has Many Names*, 52.

4. John Hick, "Jesus and the World Religions," in *The Myth of God Incarnate*, ed. John Hick and Paul Knitter (Philadelphia: Westminster Press, 1977).

5. Ibid., 179–81.

6. Ibid., 168–71.

7. Ibid., 170–71.

8. Ibid., 176.

9. Hick's use of Kant can be traced back at least to 1982 with the publication of *God Has Many Names*. In time, Hick would make use of philosophers such as Ludwig Wittgenstein as well, but without abandoning his basic Kantian view of religious experience. See Hick, *God Has Many Names*.

10. Hick, *God Has Many Names*, 67.

11. John Hick, *Problems of Religious Pluralism* (New York: St. Martin's Press, 1985).

12. Ibid., 24–25.

13. Ibid., 25.

14. John Hick, *A Christian Theology of Religions: The Rainbow of Faiths* (Louisville, Ky.: Westminster John Knox Press, 1995), 25–26.

15. Hick, *Problems of Religious Pluralism*.

16. Ibid., 34, 46, 92.

17. Ibid., 39.

18. Ibid., 39–40.

19. Ibid., 43.

20. Ibid., 88

21. Ibid., 93–95.

22. John Hick, *An Interpretation of Religion: Human Responses to the Transcendent* (New Haven: Yale University Press, 1989).

23. Ibid., 235–36.

24. For Hick's arguments against skepticism and religious exclusivism, see *An Interpretation of Religion*, 210–30.

25. Ibid., 236.

26. Ibid., 243–44.

Chapter 3

PAUL KNITTER'S LIBERATION THEOLOGY OF RELIGIONS

Along with John Hick, Paul Knitter is the figure most associated with the call for a pluralist theology of religions. In his more recent writings, Knitter has shared some of his autobiography, a story that provides a personal context for his passionately held beliefs about Christianity's need to engage the other religions honestly and openly.

Knitter describes his life as a "journey with the Other," by which he means that his life, first as a Roman Catholic missionary and then as a theologian, has led him to encounters with truths that have not easily been assimilated into his own view of the world. In fact, he speaks of two great "Others": the religious Other (the multitude of believers who follow paths other than his own Christian path) and the suffering Other (all those who have been marginalized by injustice and oppression).[1]

In the 1950s, as a seminarian, Paul Knitter was an exclusivist studying theology to bring the truth of Christianity to the world. In hindsight, he can now look back on this time of his life as a first step toward embracing the religious Other. With the beginning of the Second Vatican Council in the early 1960s, Knitter found himself in Rome. As a result of his reading of the first drafts of *Nostra Aetate* (the document on the church's relationship with other religions) and, later, under the influence of Karl Rahner, his teacher in Germany, Knitter moved from exclusivism to inclusivism. During his studies in Germany, Knitter met and befriended a Muslim student and began to wonder if his friend was really an anonymous Christian after all. His dissatisfaction with inclusivist

theologies bore fruit with the publication of his widely influential book
No Other Name? in 1985.[2] This book is concerned chiefly with the need
to revise our understanding of Jesus, our Christology, in light of the diversity of faiths. Since the publication of *No Other Name?*, Knitter has
increasingly argued for the need to incorporate the justice concerns of the
theology of liberation into Christianity's view of non-Christian religions.
The theology of liberation is a movement that started within the Catholic
Church in Latin America and has since become influential throughout the
world. Liberation theologians insist that theology should begin with reflection on the meaning of the gospel in the light of the efforts of
Christians to work for the liberation of the oppressed. Theology that does
not give a "preferential option for the poor" is theology in service of the
oppression and injustice of the status quo and not faithful to Jesus' liberating gospel of love and justice.

Every theology of religions, I have argued, has to come to grips
with two great Christian doctrines: the uniqueness of Jesus and God's
universal will to save. John Hick's Copernican revolution from
Christocentrism to theocentrism and eventually to reality-centeredness
led to important consequences regarding the way Christians understand
Jesus of Nazareth. Even more than John Hick, Paul Knitter has taken up
the problem of Christology in relation to the many religions of the world.
Hick approaches the problem of the uniqueness of Jesus with his claim
that the doctrine of the incarnation should be understood as a "myth" or
"paradigm" modeling God's action in the world. Paul Knitter is more interested in the historical Jesus and his original preaching of the kingdom
of God.[3] Knitter wants to emphasize the fact that Jesus did not preach
about himself as the incarnation. Jesus preached the liberation of every
human being in the coming of God's kingdom. In this we can see the beginnings of his concern for bringing together the theology of religions
and the political concerns of the theology of liberation.

Jesus in a Pluralistic World

How must our understanding of the role of Jesus in the salvation
of the world change if we were to adopt a theocentric understanding of
religions? If Jesus should be understood primarily as a witness to the

mystery of the divine that lies beyond us all, is faith in Jesus Christ necessary for salvation? Change is nothing new for Christianity. This has been especially true in Christianity's understanding of Jesus. Over the last twenty centuries, new historical situations have required Christians to rethink their views of Jesus as founder of their religion and as savior of the world.[4] Today Christianity must interpret the meaning of its faith in Jesus anew, now in light of the vast diversity of religious paths. Knitter argues that the basis for a more adequate understanding of Jesus can be found by returning to the New Testament and the original preaching of Jesus.

According to Paul Knitter, John Hick's call for a theocentric revolution is made all the more urgent because Jesus himself was theocentric.[5] Jesus did not preach about himself. Jesus preached about God and what God was doing to set free every human being. The theme of his preaching was the kingdom of God. There is wide agreement among scholars of the New Testament on this point. Knitter also acknowledges that most New Testament scholars are in agreement that Jesus saw himself as instrumental, in some way, in the coming of God's kingdom and that Jesus saw himself as the eschatological prophet who had come to fulfill the hopes of Israel. Nevertheless, in Knitter's view, Jesus must be seen as a witness to God and not to himself.

In contrast to the historical Jesus, the New Testament is Christocentric. If Jesus proclaimed the kingdom of God, the New Testament proclaims Jesus as Lord. Despite this fact, the original theocentric message of the historical Jesus was not lost. Paul, for example, informs his readers: "You [belong to] Christ and Christ [belongs] to God" (1 Cor 3:23). Therefore, the Christocentric language of the New Testament should never be interpreted in a way that the transcendent mystery of God comes to be eclipsed by the brightness of Christ. The best way to guard against such an error is to note two basic points. First, the New Testament does not speak about Jesus with one voice. The New Testament contains multiple views of Jesus and his role in the salvation of the world. Second, we must remember that statements in the New Testament regarding Jesus are always poetic or metaphoric and not to be taken literally.[6] For example, the many titles given to Jesus in the New Testament, such as Lord, Son of Man, Word of God, and Messiah, are interpretations of the meaning of Jesus, not definitions that are exhaustive.

With these two points in mind, Knitter argues that the long history of Christianity's quest to understand Jesus is evolutionary, not developmental. Knitter's definition of these terms is crucial to his point. In a developmental scheme, all that can come to be is already present at the beginning, at least implicitly. In an evolutionary scheme, the genuinely new and unforeseen is possible.[7] Since the church's Christology is evolutionary and not merely developmental, no understanding of Jesus should be set in stone as absolute and unchangeable. Today the evolution of Christianity's understanding of Jesus should continue through dialogue with non-Christian believers. Most of all, Knitter believes that Christians can remain faithful to the mission of the historical Jesus by returning to his original theocentric witness to the kingdom of God.[8]

The Uniqueness of Jesus in the New Testament

When Knitter points out that no understanding of Jesus should be allowed to become absolute and unchanging, he includes even the New Testament's own witness to Jesus. More accurately, one must say the multiple views of Jesus found in the New Testament, for the New Testament does not speak with one unified voice about Jesus. One New Testament claim about Jesus that is in need of revision has to do with his uniqueness as the savior of the world.

The New Testament's recognition of Jesus as the unique savior of the world is undeniable. Jesus is extolled as the "one mediator between God and the human race" (1 Tm 2:5). Since Jesus claims that no one "comes to the Father except through me" (Jn 14:6), then there can be "no other name" (Acts 4:12) through which we can be saved. If the uniqueness of Jesus for the authors of the New Testament cannot be denied, neither should we lose track of the tentative, time-conditioned character of these statements about Jesus. How are we to understand the New Testament in a way that is adequate for the needs of Christians today?

There are many reasons why this kind of "one and only" language would be so prominent in the New Testament. The New Testament, Knitter argues, was composed in an era very different from our own. All the New Testament authors presumed that truth is final, unchanging, and absolute. The notion that their interpretation of Jesus might develop, let alone evolve, over time was not a cultural presupposition for the New Testament authors.

In addition, early Christians did not think that there was very much time. The books of the New Testament reflect, in different degrees, the early Christian community's belief that Jesus would return and history would end very soon. As a Jew, Jesus himself expected the fulfillment of God's plan to happen in Jerusalem with the coming of the kingdom of God. Not surprisingly, therefore, since Jesus is seen as the one who inaugurates the end-days of God's plan for the world, he is also seen as the final and unsurpassable revelation of God in the New Testament. In the resurrection of the Lord, the new and final age has dawned. This outlook, according to Knitter, need not become absolutely normative for modern Christians; they can affirm the importance of Jesus without falling into an exclusivist understanding of Jesus as savior.

A third explanation for the "one and only" language about Jesus in the New Testament has to do with the political and social situation of the early Christian community. When the New Testament was being composed in the first century, Christians constituted a tiny and beleaguered minority group. Claims regarding the unsurpassable greatness of Jesus had a social and institutional function within the community: these claims strengthened the fragile faith of the early Christians and helped them to persevere in the face of persecution. This means that the absolute claims the New Testament makes about Jesus reflect a specific historical era that now is past. For Knitter, this also means that contemporary Christians should now place these absolute claims within their historical context. They are not proper for the church today.

In short, Knitter believes that New Testament claims about the uniqueness of Jesus tell us more about the early church than about the reality of Jesus. These passages should be seen as proclamations of the early Christian community's unswerving faith. They need not be taken as definitive. In these passages, we find the poetic and spontaneous language of religious faith shaped in large part by historical circumstances very different from our own, not the precise language of defined doctrines.[9]

Knitter's discussion of the New Testament and its statements about the uniqueness of Jesus as a savior parallels John Hick's view of the incarnation as a metaphor or myth.[10] Christian teaching that Jesus Christ is both divine and human should be thought of as one possible model for understanding salvation, but not the only possible model. As a religious teaching, the incarnation is to be taken seriously, but not literally and not exclusively as the only possible way human beings can be saved. The Word becoming flesh is not a literal historical event that pertains to Jesus of Nazareth, a single individual. The incarnation is a way of imagining the ultimate unity of God with all creation. Somewhat similarly, Knitter thinks we should take New Testament statements about the uniqueness of Jesus seriously but not literally. Once these statements are understood as the products of social and historical circumstances very different from our own, we can appreciate them for what they are: statements of the Christian community's deep faith in Jesus and their commitment to continuing his mission to proclaim the kingdom of God. We need not take them as absolutely normative for us today. We can continue that faith and that commitment without taking this language literally.

Knitter then follows Hick in taking the next step. What Christians see in Jesus, they can see in other religious figures. There can be other incarnations of God's presence in the world besides Jesus. Why, argues Knitter, should we believe that God's offer of grace has been given only once in the entire history of the human race? Why would the possibility of there being other saviors denigrate Jesus as a savior? Jesus is a witness to what God has done for the entire human race. He preached the kingdom of God, not himself as the one and only incarnation of God. Today Christians need to enter into dialogue with non-Christians to discover how the salvation they see in the way of Jesus is also available in the way of the Buddha and the other religions.

The Uniqueness of Jesus for Today

A Christology adequate for today, an understanding of Jesus that meets the needs of Christian believers in a world of religious diversity, must emphasize Jesus' original proclamation of the coming kingdom of God, according to Knitter. Focusing on the message preached instead of on the preacher of the message will bring Christians back to the original, liberating truth of the kingdom of God, with its social, economic, and political implications. In order to accomplish this end, to paraphrase Lenin, some eggs may have to be broken.

In order to return to Jesus' original message, Knitter believes Christians will have to recognize the fact that some teachings that were once useful have now become obsolete and even burdensome for the church. Traditional teachings about the unsurpassed uniqueness of Jesus as the sole savior of the world, for example, "are possibly nurtured more by the desire to maintain power and privilege than by the desire to promote truth and freedom."[11] By submitting their beliefs to the test of Jesus' mission to announce the kingdom of God, the self-serving nature of some Christian doctrines will come to light. The priority of Christians today should not be to protect traditional teaching about the unparalleled uniqueness of Jesus, but rather to clarify what the kingdom of God might mean for the world today.

Knitter's critical view of traditional teaching regarding the uniqueness of Jesus leads to some significant implications. First, if Christians are to continue to believe that Jesus makes salvation available to all, they must realize that this can be true only to the extent that the disciples of Jesus today are trying to make God's kingdom of justice and reconciliation a concrete reality throughout the world. Second, since this is not yet the case, there is no basis for claiming that Jesus is the final, unsurpassable savior of the world. In actual fact, there are as yet many for whom Jesus does not signify God's liberating love.[12] Third, if absolute claims about Jesus are not possible, neither are they necessary. Christians should not become entangled in useless arguments about Jesus as the final and unsurpassable revelation of God. Instead, as disciples, Christians should do what Jesus did: work for bringing about God's justice for the poor and oppressed in the world. Finally, a renewed emphasis on Jesus' preaching of the kingdom means that Christians should be more attentive to signs worldwide that the justice and peace God has planned for creation are coming about. This means that Christians must recognize at least the possibility that there are other saviors, other incarnations, other revelations from God in the world. By sitting down with non-Christians at a dialogue table, they may discover religious paths equal to Christianity.

The Resurrection: Proof of Jesus' Uniqueness?

Jesus, unlike other religious figures, was raised from the dead. Some Christians are quick to point this out in discussions with non-Christians. Does the "fact" of the resurrection make Jesus the unique and unsurpassed savior of the world? Does it make Christianity the only true religion?

There is wide agreement among modern scholars of the New Testament that the resurrection should be thought of as neither a purely subjective event "within" the disciples nor as a literal, objective event "in front of" the disciples.[13] In the quest for a "proof" that Jesus was really God and that Christianity is in fact true, some have insisted that the resurrection be thought of as an objective historical event, an irrefutable and observable "fact." Others, in the hope of protecting belief in the resurrection from the criticism of modern skeptics, have argued that the resurrection is a purely subjective event that went on within the disciples. In this view, Jesus may be said to have risen figuratively in the hearts of the disciples in the form of their renewed resolve to keep alive the memory of their slain Lord.

Following these scripture scholars, Knitter suggests that we steer a difficult middle course between these two alternatives. The resurrection is not an observable historical event that can be known by anyone. That Christ is risen from the dead is not known objectively, by looking at the empty tomb, for example. In the New Testament, the disciples understand that Jesus is risen from the dead only by undergoing their own dramatic religious transformation (*metanoia*). After the death of Jesus, something powerful and transformative happened to the disciples that led them to proclaim that Jesus had been "raised up." Take, for example, the story of the appearance of the Risen Lord on the road to Emmaus (Lk 24:13–35). In this famous story, the disciples are aware from the beginning that the tomb of Jesus is empty. But this knowledge produces only confusion in them. The disciples realize that Jesus is risen from the dead only in "the breaking of the bread." The Emmaus story is really about the Eucharist as a religiously transforming celebration. Today, when Christians gather for the breaking of the bread and are touched by the power of God, they too say Christ "has risen."

The resurrection is not a unique historical event that proves that

Jesus really was the Messiah. The resurrection is a way of speaking about a profound religious transformation that takes place within Christians, but not only within Christians. The Christian term for this spiritual transformation is *resurrection*. Hindus, Muslims, and others have their own way of naming this experience. Knitter offers a specific example. After the death of Siddhartha Gautama, the historical Buddha, his disciples also underwent a conversion experience that led them to experience the Lord Buddha's continued presence in the world. Of course, Buddhists do not talk about this conversion experience using the metaphor of "resurrection." They have other metaphors. *Resurrection* is a term Christians have chosen to express their experience of spiritual transformation.

If the resurrection is understood properly and not as a "proof" that Jesus is divine, Christians can succeed in developing an understanding of Jesus that does not make absolute claims for the superiority of their own religion.[14]

A Theocentric Faith

With this interpretation of Jesus, Knitter believes that Christians can endorse a pluralistic theology of religions based on John Hick's theocentric approach to religious diversity.[15] A pluralistic theology of religions does not jeopardize a Christian's faith in Jesus Christ. The possibility of there being other saviors, saviors recognized in non-Christian religions, may produce confusion and anxiety in Christian believers. This anxiety, however, is rooted in a misplaced trust in doctrines and institutions that are historically conditioned and not central to belief in Jesus. In fact, Knitter believes that a theocentric understanding of Jesus can even deepen and purify our faith in Jesus by returning our focus to the work of Jesus in proclaiming the good news of the kingdom. A true and mature faith in Jesus and his message does not require us to believe that Jesus is the only savior known to human beings any more than the true and mature love of a spouse requires one to reject the fact that there are other women or men in the world who are as beautiful or noble as one's spouse. Openness to others should be taken as a sign of depth and maturity.

Like John Hick, Knitter's commitment to a pluralistic theology of religions requires him to expand greatly his understanding of this perplexing word, *salvation*. Karl Rahner believed that salvation can be found beyond the institutional boundaries of Christianity. But in Rahner's inclusivist view, salvation must always be understood as the victory of God's eternal life over sin and death realized in the resurrection of Jesus Christ. Paul Knitter would have us believe that the Christian view of salvation in Christ is but one way of understanding what is a more general occurrence in all the great religious traditions of the world. What Christians call eternal life, Buddhists call Nirvana. Christians may speak of the resurrection of the body and the kingdom of God. Hindus speak of being released (*moksa*) from samsara and the unity of the soul (*atman*) with ultimate reality itself (*brahman*). All these images must now be included in the general category of "salvation."

Therefore, Christians should maintain their commitment to Jesus but combine this commitment with a genuine openness to the truths of other religious paths. To accomplish this task, Knitter points out that it is helpful to keep in mind the creative tension that exists between the universality and particularity of every religious experience of salvation. Salvation is universal in that the salvation that Christians know through Jesus Christ is available to human beings in any number of ways, including ways as yet unknown to most Christians. Salvation is also particular in that it is never available to human beings in a general or abstract way. Salvation is always available in the form of a particular path, practice, sacrament, ritual, or savior figure. Jesus Christ is but one particular instance of salvation. But since salvation always becomes real and accessible for a human being in a particular, limited way, naturally human beings are subject to the temptation to make absolute what is but a particular manifestation of salvation. Since "Jesus is decisive for me," Christians are led to conclude that "Jesus must be decisive for everyone." In order to remain committed to Jesus and yet open to the truths of other religious traditions, Christians must not lose sight of the tension between the particular and the universal that is present in every genuine religious experience of salvation. To make a particular manifestation of salvation absolute for all is to fashion an idol out of what is only a particular manifestation of truth. To insist that

Jesus is the one and only unsurpassable savior of all is to fall prey to this idolatry.

A theocentric faith in Jesus and his witness to God therefore requires what Knitter calls an "open-ended confession." The term is taken from H. Richard Niebuhr.[16] In dealing with non-Christian believers, Christians should explain, simply and humbly, what Jesus has done for them without making extravagant and unwarranted claims about his uniqueness and the superiority of Christianity over other religions. All the rest should be left to God. Building on Niebuhr, Knitter believes that this open-ended confession of Jesus allows Christians to remain completely committed to following in the life and mission of Jesus while remaining open to a recognition of what God has accomplished in other religions.

> A confessional approach, then, will be both certain and open-ended. It will enable Christians to take a firm position; but it will also require them to be open to and possibly learn from other positions. It will allow them to affirm the uniqueness and the universal significance of what God has done in Jesus; but at the same time it will require them to recognize and be challenged by the uniqueness and universal significance of what the divine mystery may have revealed through others. In boldly proclaiming that God has indeed been defined in Jesus, Christians will also humbly admit that God has not been confined to Jesus.[17]

Jesus, therefore, is unique. There is no savior like him. Christians, however, must also recognize that the historical Buddha is likewise a unique and unparalleled savior and that there is no other savior like him either.

A Liberation Theology of Religions

Paul Knitter's view of religious diversity, perhaps even more than John Hick's, has been in a constant state of revision in response not only to his critics but also to his work for social justice both here in the United States and abroad. In *No Other Name?* Knitter's debt to feminist and liberationist theologians such as Rosemary Radford Ruether, Leonardo Boff, and Jon Sobrino is evident. After *No Other Name?*

Knitter's commitment to responding to the problem of religious diversity from the perspective of the theology of liberation has become even more pronounced. Two years after the publication of *No Other Name?*, Knitter worked with John Hick in putting together a collection of essays entitled *The Myth of Christian Uniqueness* on the subject of a pluralistic theology of religions. This book included an essay by Knitter himself, one of his most important contributions to the pluralist debate, entitled, "Toward a Liberationist Theology of Religions."[18] This essay was eventually followed by the publication of two books, both of which confirm his "liberationist turn" in developing a pluralistic theology of religions: *One Earth Many Religions* appeared in 1995; *Jesus and the Other Names* appeared in 1996.[19]

Paul Knitter believes very strongly that the theology of liberation and the theology of religions need each other. The theology of liberation, emerging as it has in the church of Latin America and its struggles with poverty and dependence, has been greatly affected by Marxist thought and its call for social transformation. Marxists, however, do not adequately understand what a driving force religion can be in bringing about social change. The theology of religions, to the extent that it calls Christians to dialogue seriously with non-Christian believers, will give liberation theologians a better sense of how religions can be forces for justice in the world.

Likewise, the theology of religions needs a greater awareness of the concerns of the theology of liberation. Knitter is emphatic in his insistence that any interreligious dialogue that ignores the problem of injustice is "a purely mystical pursuit" or merely a "pastime" for academics. In dialogues that are limited to theological abstractions, something essential is missing. A pluralistic theology of religions that leads us to turn a blind eye to injustice and oppression has naively let itself become an ideology in service of the status quo. Seen from the perspective of the theology of liberation, the primary purpose of interreligious dialogue and a pluralistic theology of religions is not to promote tolerance but rather to bring the many religions together in the joint effort to address the reality of suffering and to bring about structural changes for economic and social justice.[20]

Bringing the theology of liberation's concern for justice to bear in the development of a pluralistic theology of religions also helps Paul

Knitter respond to some of the concerns his critics raised against his earlier work. If a pluralistic theology of religions requires Christians to surrender their absolute claims about Jesus and to recognize the possibility of there being other saviors, does this not imply that all religions are relative? Is any religion as good as any other? Liberation theology's insistence on the primacy of justice and the need for social change allows Knitter to make judgments about religions.

Liberation theologians have been especially forceful in underscoring the dangers courted when a religion becomes merely a support for an unjust status quo. When the social effect of religious teaching is to support those in power and to keep the poor powerless, religious doctrine has become an ideology. In this case, what religions call "God's will" is in fact the will of the rich and powerful in disguise. The theology of liberation reminds us that even the most fundamental of "orthodox" doctrines must be judged by the fruit they bear. Religious teachings that yield oppressive fruit need to be exposed and rejected. Knitter offers Christian doctrines regarding the uniqueness of Jesus as an example. The cozy partnership between the Christian missionary effort and Western imperialism becomes much easier to explain when we remember Christianity's belief that human beings can be saved only through faith in Jesus. Christian belief in the uniqueness of Christ has been used to justify the domination and exploitation of the "heathens." Inclusivist theologies of religion, where the truth revealed in Jesus is asserted to be found in non-Christian religions as well, are analogous to First World calls for "economic development," which actually perpetuate the dependence of Third World peoples on the industrialized economies of the First World.[21]

Common Ground for Dialogue—Sōtéria

What do religions have in common? What makes mutual understanding and cooperation between religious traditions possible? John Hick in both his earlier and later contributions to the debate regarding a pluralistic theology of religions has turned to a transcendent metaphysical truth that he recognizes as common to all the religions. In his early work, he spoke of "the divine mystery" that lies transcendently beyond all the various religious expressions of it. In his later work, in an effort to be more inclusive of religions like Daoism and Theravada Buddhism, which are not centered on a personal divinity, Hick speaks of "the Real." Paul Knitter believes that social justice concerns also provide a common basis for interreligious understanding.

Thus, Knitter believes he has found a basis for interreligious dialogue in the theology of liberation. From a liberationist perspective, all religions *should* be concerned with the plight of the poor. Liberation theologians hold that the experience of the poor and solidarity with their plight provide the proper perspective for understanding the Bible. Knitter builds on this insight when he notes that the experience of the poor also provides us with the proper basis for understanding the universe of faiths.[22]

> If the religions of the world, in other words, can recognize poverty and oppression as a common problem, if they can share a common commitment (expressed in different forms) to remove such evils, they will have the basis for reaching across their incommensurabilities and differences in order to hear and understand each other and possibly be transformed in the process.[23]

Concern for the poor, Knitter cautions, should not be taken as the "essence" of all religions. Attention to the voices of the poor and oppressed constitute only a useful starting point for dialogue, an issue that, whether religious believers realize it or not, forms the proper context for the encounter of religions today.

The problem of injustice cuts across cultures and religions. As no religion has a monopoly on concern for the poor, so also no religion can exempt itself from the ethical demand to respond to the cry of the poor. In light of these considerations taken from the theology of liberation, Knitter admits that his earlier ideas regarding a pluralistic theology of religions need to be amended. In *No Other Name?*, Knitter heeded John Hick's call for a "Copernican revolution" to a theocentric view of all the great religious traditions of the world. For Christians this would mean moving from the idea that Christ is the one and only incarnation of God within the entire history of the human race (Christocentrism) to the idea that Jesus is a witness to the saving power of the one, mysterious God witnessed to by all the great religions of the world (theocentrism). But as a result of his own dialogue with the liberation theologians (and even more recently with those most concerned with the ecological well-being of the earth), Paul Knitter has turned from his theocentric model to what he now calls a "soteriocentric" model.

The central truth that links together all the religions and provides a basis for their coming together in dialogue is *sōtéria*, which Knitter defines as "the well being of human beings and the earth," or "the ineffable mystery of salvation."[24] The basis for interreligious dialogue cannot be how religious believers all meet in Christ (even implicitly), as in Karl Rahner's theology of the anonymous Christian. Neither can the basis for dialogue be in how all human beings are related to the transcendent divine mystery (theocentrism). Real dialogue between religious believers, according to Knitter, is possible to the extent that these believers "are engaged in promoting human welfare and bringing about liberation with and for the poor and nonpersons."[25]

Religions imagine ultimate reality in a multitude of different ways, monotheistically, polytheistically, as a personal divinity or impersonal principle. Religions are all different in the way they speak of their religious experience. What religions have in common, despite their many differences, is their concern for liberation. As a ground dialogue, *sōtéria* is a good place to start, but it will constantly be shifting and clarifying itself as the dialogues proceed. The advantage Knitter sees in moving from theocentrism to the experience of salvation as a common element linking religions is the need to avoid imposing Western notions of God on the other religions at the dialogue table.[26]

Knitter believes that a concern to explore the reality of *sōtéria* should provide all religions with the ability to enter into dialogue with other religions. Religious believers have more in common in their quest for liberation than in their religious doctrines. In Christianity, *sōtéria* is present in terms of Jesus' proclamation of the kingdom of God. In other religions, *sōtéria* is expressed in different ways. This means that *sōtéria* is no more than a "shaky ground," a suitable starting point for serious dialogue between the religions of the world.

The Problem of Relativism

A problem endemic to pluralist theologies of religion is relativism. If all religions, potentially at least, can lead a believer to reality-centeredness, is every religion as good as every other religion? Why then be a Christian or Muslim or Buddhist? If all religions, more or less, are salvific to the extent that they make *sōtéria* available to their followers, is any religion distinct in any significant way from any other religion? In order to live responsibly with the intrusive fact of religious diversity today, religious believers need not only to understand the teachings and mores of those who follow other religious paths, they need to be able to judge the value and effectiveness of these other religious paths as well.[27]

In proposing a way for judging the value and effectiveness of religions in making salvation available to their adherents, Knitter knows that he is venturing into a real minefield. In addressing an issue such as this, a pluralistic theology of religions can easily fall back into the theological imperialism and cultural insensitivity they complain about in exclusivist and inclusivist theologies. From the perspective of Knitter's deep commitments to social justice, the danger here would be to promote a theology of religions that may seem pluralistic on the surface, but may amount to nothing more than a theological form of neo-colonialism.[28] With all these dangers in mind, Knitter still believes that *sōtéria* can be used as a basis for evaluating religions.

Religions need to be called to account for their actions and the quality of the justice they promote. Nevertheless, the standard for making such judgments about religions, according to Knitter, is not monopolized by any particular religion. The basis for judging religions cuts across religious traditions. Here Knitter is making a claim with some very far-reaching implications. By placing his money on the "well being of the poor and non-persons" as the central value for evaluating religions, Knitter is suggesting that the real differences that distinguish religious believers are not theoretical or doctrinal but ethical. Furthermore, Buddhists and Muslims, Christians and Confucians who are committed to justice may well have more in common with one another than they do with their own coreligionists who do not have such commitments. The turn to *sōtéria* clarifies not only the real differences that distinguish one religion from another but also the real differences between believers from within the same tradition. This is all the more true when we note the distinctly social and political meaning *sotéria* has for Paul Knitter.[29]

Recognizing the paramount importance of social justice for all religions is Knitter's way to combat relativism. This effect will be clearly seen when religious believers enter into dialogue with one another. Christians, for example, should put aside their traditional claims about Jesus as the unique savior of the world and make Jesus' proclamation of the kingdom of God their central priority in interreligious dialogue. This shift in concern will help transform dialogue from being a merely academic exercise for elites to being a concrete way for bringing about the righteousness and justice of God's kingdom on earth. Knitter quotes theologian Harvey Cox approvingly.

> Similarities and differences which once seemed important fade away as the real differences—between those whose sacred stories are used to perpetuate domination and those whose religion strengthens them for the fight against domination—emerge more clearly.[30]

When it comes to being religious, the real dividing line increasingly will be drawn not between religious traditions, as it is today, but across religious traditions. The most dramatic religious differences will be between those who work to perpetuate oppression and those who have found salvation by working to end it. *Sotéria* is present and at work in the world today in many ways. The hope Christians have in the coming kingdom of God is but one way *sotéria* is manifest in the world. No manifestation of *sotéria* is absolute.

Jesus Christ, Liberator

If a liberationist approach to a pluralist theology of religions is helpful in addressing the problem of relativism, yet another advantage of a liberationist approach has to do with the knotty problem of traditional Christian claims about the unsurpassed uniqueness of Christ. "In order to avoid preestablished absolutist positions that prevent a genuinely pluralistic dialogue," Knitter argues, "Christians must, it seems, re-vamp or even reject their traditional understanding of Jesus Christ as God's final, definitive, normative voice."[31] The theology of liberation, when applied to the reality of religious diversity and the need for a plu-ralistic theology of religions, can help in this matter.

Liberation theologians have argued that religious doctrine must be judged by the social fruit it bears. More to the point at hand, these same theologians have also argued that only those who are engaged concretely in social action in the cause of liberation are in a position to interpret the true meaning of religious doctrine. We do not first know the truth and then put it into practice. By engaging in social action as a response to the call of the gospel, we begin to know the truth of Jesus Christ. Those who are not actively involved in opposing injustice tend to interpret religious doctrine ideologically in ways that support the power of those who oppress the poor and the weak and exploit the earth. Knitter applies these ideas to the problem of the uniqueness of Jesus.[32]

Since the meaning of Christian doctrine becomes apparent by means of action in the name of liberation, concrete social action in the name of the gospel is the best basis for understanding the saving role of Jesus Christ. The numerous titles that name the mystery of Christ in the New Testament (Son of God, Son of Man, Lord, Messiah, etc.) are not the result of abstract speculation. These early interpretations of the meaning of the life and death of Jesus arose out of the early Christian community's experience of discipleship in the name of Jesus and the kingdom he preached.[33] As Knitter argued in *No Other Name?*, no un-derstanding of Christ should be taken as absolute and final—even the New Testament's understanding of Jesus as the unique and unsurpass-able savior. The uniqueness of Jesus can be understood for Christians today only from the perspective of solidarity with the poor and social action with the poor.

Liberation theologians like Jon Sobrino have argued that if Christians want to believe that Jesus Christ is good news for every human being in the world, then they must recognize that this is not true simply because traditional doctrines have asserted it to be true. Jesus Christ can be good news for the whole world and for every human being in the world only to the extent that this good news becomes concretely embodied in the liberating social action of Christians in all parts of the world.[34] Knitter takes Sobrino's thought a step further. In facing the reality of religious diversity honestly, Christians may find a multitude of ways different religions have of working for the liberation of the world and its many oppressed peoples. This brings Knitter to a major conclusion regarding the importance of interreligious dialogue.

> This means, concretely, that unless we are engaged in the *praxis of Christian dialogue* with other religions—following Christ, applying his message, within the dialogue with other believers—we cannot experience and confirm what the uniqueness and normativity of Christ means.[35]

In other words, dialogue with other religious traditions is essential in the continued evolution of Christianity's understanding of Jesus and its own mission to witness to the liberation of the world in the coming of the kingdom of God. But since dialogue with other religions is only beginning, Christians have no basis for continuing to teach that Jesus is the one, final, and unsurpassable savior of all.

If *sōtéria* is to be recognized as the basis for judging religions, then Christians must also recognize that the soteriocentric approach suggested by the melding of liberation theology and the pluralistic theology of religions is also the basis for judging the claims of Christianity as well. Here Knitter wants to include Christianity's claims about the uniqueness of Jesus as the one, unsurpassable savior of the world. By submitting their own religious tradition to the test of dialogue with other religious traditions on the issue of liberation and the ecological well-being of the earth, a number of possibilities arise for Christians. On the one hand, Christians may be confronted with the need to revise what they thought previously about Jesus as savior of the world. On the other hand, this may not turn out to be the case. In his proclamation of the kingdom of justice and peace, Jesus may prove to be unsurpassed as the liberator of the earth. Or perhaps Christians may come to recognize other ways to liberation equal to the liberation revealed by Jesus.

Universal, Decisive, Indispensable

In one of his most recent contributions to the debate over a pluralistic theology of religions, "Five Theses on the Uniqueness of Jesus," Paul Knitter has raised the eyebrows of many by stating forthrightly his view that faith in Jesus as a savior figure with universal significance is "indispensable."[36] John Hick has criticized this claim by accusing Knitter of abandoning pluralism and returning to a form of inclusivism. Knitter is clearly trying to present his notion of a pluralistic theology of religions in a way that is as inoffensive as possible to tradition-minded Christians. As a savior, Jesus is unique. The real question for Christians is to understand *how* Jesus is unique and how Jesus' uniqueness is related to the unique characteristics of other saviors. He wants to show how Christians can understand Jesus' own uniqueness in a way that is faithful to the mission and message of Christ but also open to the unique truths of the other faiths.

Knitter prefaces his statement about the indispensability of Jesus by reasserting his earlier position that, when Christians say that Jesus is truly the savior of the world, *truly* doesn't mean "only."[37] To believe, as Christians do, that Jesus is truly a savior of the world does not imply that Jesus is the only savior of the world. Thus, contrary to traditional doctrines, Christian faith does not require Christians to assert that Jesus, as a revelation from God, is full, definitive, and unsurpassable.[38] In Jesus, Christians have no monopoly on the revelation of God. In Knitter's view, no finite individual can exhaust the fullness of the Infinite. To identify the finite with the Infinite uncritically is idolatry. Does this imply that the doctrine of the incarnation is idolatry?

Knitter defends the doctrine of the incarnation but not its traditional interpretation. Jesus represents God's presence within the world but does not exhaust it. The point of Christianity's teaching that Jesus was both divine and human is to affirm that divinity has taken on the fullness of our humanity. This affirmation, however, does not make Jesus the only way this truth can be affirmed. In Jesus, the fullness of God is present within the world as a particular, historical individual but not in any exclusive way.

Thus, if Christians want to affirm that the Divine has truly been "made flesh" in Jesus, they cannot, at the same time, hold that the

> Divine has *absolutely* or *totally* been made flesh in Jesus. Flesh
> cannot be made into a total container of the Divine.[39]

In Jesus, God is manifest fully, but this does not imply that we have ever
grasped the fullness of God.[40] Similarly, Jesus is not the definitive Word
of God, at least if definitive means that nothing essentially new can be
said about God after Jesus.[41] Christian faith is eschatological—revelation
continues until the fullness of time when God will be "all in all." And neither is Jesus the unsurpassable revelation of God, for God is perfectly
capable of revealing more of his fullness at different times and places.

But if Jesus is neither full, definitive, nor unsurpassable, Knitter believes that Christians must proclaim boldly to their non-Christian neighbors that Jesus is universal, decisive, and, as noted above, indispensable.[42]
Jesus is universal in that in Jesus there is a revelation of God's saving
truth that is of significance to human beings no matter what their cultural background or religious commitments might be. In Jesus the truth
of God's plan for creation becomes manifest within time in such a way
that all peoples can witness to this revelation and respond to it.

Jesus is decisive in that the truth revealed in his proclamation of
the kingdom literally calls us to make an irrevocable decision about
ourselves and the way we are going to spend our lives in this world.
This decision for or against the kingdom may very well require us to
decide against other paths and commitments. In this regard, Knitter
even refers to Jesus as "normative" and recognizes that rejecting such a
view in *No Other Name?* was an error.[43] By "normative," Knitter does
not mean that God's revelation in Jesus is unsurpassable. Jesus is normative in the sense that the truth revealed through Jesus requires
Christians and non-Christians alike to change their lives. Jesus is not
normative in the sense of being God's only call to reform our lives and
work for the well-being of humankind and the earth.

Finally, Knitter believes that God's truth made known in Jesus is
indispensable.

> Thus, it seems to me that, inherent in the Christian experience of
> Jesus is the conviction that those who have not known and in
> some way accepted the message and power of the gospel are
> missing something in their knowledge and living of truth.

75

> Whatever truth about the Ultimate and the human condition there may be in other religious traditions, such truth can be enhanced and clarified through an encounter with the good news made known in Jesus. In a qualified, but real sense, persons of other religious paths are "unfulfilled" without Christ.[44]

Jesus may not be God's full, definitive, and unsurpassable truth. All the same, Jesus proclaims a (not *the*) universal, decisive, and indispensable message.

*   *   *

Knitter is certainly not a relativist. His strong commitment to following out the implications of bringing the theology of religions together with the theology of liberation provides a clear and decisive criterion for separating the religious sheep from the goats. In fact, in his latest writings, Knitter has become increasingly clear about what makes a religion true and what leads to the salvation of human beings and the earth. Paul Knitter's earlier works seem to suggest an affinity with John Hick's more philosophical program for a pluralistic theology of religions. I believe this seeming affinity is misleading. Knitter's interest in basing his pluralistic theology of religions on the theology of liberation is visible in his early work. Knitter's commitment to liberation is what is leading him, currently, to part company with John Hick. Knitter's commitment to the political implications of the theology of liberation has led him increasingly to a recognition of the "indispensability" of faith in Jesus, the Liberator. This means that Knitter's view of religious diversity is very much different from that of Hick. At the very least, Knitter's liberationist approach to religious diversity indicates that pluralistic theologies of religions are not all cut from the same bolt of cloth. In the following chapter, we will look at other options for a pluralist theology of religions that differ in their own ways from both John Hick and Paul Knitter.

NOTES

1. Paul Knitter, *One Earth Many Religions: Multifaith Dialogue and Global Responsibility* (Maryknoll, N.Y.: Orbis Books, 1995), 1–8.

2. Paul Knitter, *No Other Name? A Critical Survey of Christian Attitudes Toward the World Religions* (Maryknoll, N.Y.: Orbis Books, 1985).

3. Ibid., 172.

4. For a fine account of how our understanding of Jesus has changed over time, see Jaroslav Pelikan, *Jesus Through the Centuries* (New York: Harper & Row, 1985).

5. Knitter, *No Other Name?*, 173.

6. Here Knitter's view of New Testament statements about Jesus runs parallel to John Hick's view of the incarnation as "myth."

7. Knitter, *No Other Name?*, 179.

8. Ibid., 180.

9. Ibid., 183–84.

10. Ibid., 190–92.

11. Ibid., 194.

12. Ibid., 195–97.

13. Ibid., 197. Among the interpreters of the New Testament named are Edward Schillebeeckx, Norman Perrin, Reginald Fuller, James Mackey, Hans Küng, Bruce Vawter, and Dermot Lane.

14. Knitter, *No Other Name?*, 200.

15. At the time that Knitter published *No Other Name?*, John Hick had not yet moved from theocentrism to reality-centeredness.

16. Knitter, *No Other Name?*, 203.

17. Ibid., 203–4.

18. Paul Knitter, "Toward a Liberationist Theology of Religions" in *The Myth of Christian Uniqueness*, ed. Paul Knitter and John Hick (Maryknoll, N.Y.: Orbis Books, 1987), 178–200.

19. Both published by Orbis Books, Maryknoll, New York.

20. Knitter, "Toward a Liberationist Theology of Religions," 179–81.

21. Ibid., 183.

22. Knitter, *One Earth Many Religions*, 54–72, 87–96.

23. Knitter, "Toward a Liberationist Theology of Religions," 185–86.

24. Ibid., 187. Knitter is citing Aloysius Pieris's article "Speaking of the Son of God in non-Christian Cultures, e.g. in Asia," in *Jesus, Son of God?*, ed. E. Schillebeeckx and J. Metz, *Concilium* 153 (New York: Seabury, 1982), 67. See also Knitter, *One Earth Many Religions*, 36, 79–82.

25. Knitter, "Toward a Liberationist Theology of Religions," 187.

26. Ibid. Notice that Knitter's move from theocentrism to soteriocentrism is parallel to John Hick's move from theocentrism to reality-centeredness. Hick's search for a common denominator linking all religions required him to come up with a concept that could include not only the Christian understanding of God but also nonpersonal ideas of the ultimate, such as the Buddha Nature and the Dao.

27. John Hick has recognized this point as well and has given a great deal of attention to the matter. See, for example, John Hick, *An Interpretation of Religion* (New Haven: Yale University Press, 1989), 299–342.

28. Knitter, "Toward a Liberationist Theology of Religions," 189.

29. Knitter, *One Earth Many Religions*, 109–11.

30. Knitter, "Toward a Liberationist Theology of Religions," 188. For the original text, see Harvey Cox, *Religion in the Secular City: Toward a Postmodern Theology* (New York: Simon & Schuster, 1984), 238.

31. Knitter, "Toward a Liberationist Theology of Religions," 191.

32. Knitter, *Jesus and the Other Names*, 65–67.

33. Ibid., 67–71.

34. In this regard, Knitter cites Jon Sobrino, *Christology at the Crossroads* (Maryknoll, N.Y.: Orbis Books, 1984), 9–10.

35. Knitter, "Toward a Liberationist Theology of Religions," 191–92.

36. The essay "Five Theses Regarding the Uniqueness of Jesus" is included with several responses to it in *The Uniqueness of Jesus: A Dialogue with Paul F. Knitter,* ed. Leonard Swidler and Paul Mojzes (Maryknoll, N.Y.: Orbis Books, 1997), 3–16. The claim regarding Jesus' indispensability for salvation can also be found in *Jesus and the Other Names,* 72.

37. Knitter, *Jesus and the Other Names,* 72; idem, "Five Theses Regarding the Uniqueness of Jesus," 7.

38. Knitter, *Jesus and the Other Names,* 73; idem, "Five Theses Regarding the Uniqueness of Jesus," 7–9.

39. Knitter, "Five Theses Regarding the Uniqueness of Jesus," 73.

40. Ibid., 74.

41. Ibid., 74–75.

42. Knitter, *Jesus and the Other Names,* 76; idem, "Five Theses Regarding the Uniqueness of Jesus," 9–11.

43. Knitter, "Five Theses Regarding the Uniqueness of Jesus," 9.

44. Ibid., 10.

Chapter 4

OTHER PLURALIST VOICES

As should be clear from our treatment of John Hick and Paul Knitter, pluralistic theologies of religion bear a family resemblance to one another. Nevertheless, they are not all the same in their presuppositions and arguments. John Hick generally prefers to think philosophically. His appeal to Kant's understanding of knowledge is an indication of his philosophical interests. Philosophy, however, is not the only way to secure a foundation for a pluralistic approach to the reality of religious diversity today. Paul Knitter's interests are more theological than philosophical. Wilfred Cantwell Smith, whose plea for a "world theology" we will discuss in this chapter, is fundamentally a historian. Both John Hick and Paul Knitter work out of a Western Christian context. Asian Christians are also contributing to the notion of a pluralistic theology of religions. In addition to the work of Wilfred Cantwell Smith, this chapter will look at Stanley Samartha, a Christian from India.

Wilfred Cantwell Smith

As a professor of the comparative history of religion at Harvard and a respected Islamicist, Wilfred Cantwell Smith has been face to face with the fact of religious diversity for decades. He is the author of several widely influential books, including *The Meaning and End of Religion* (1964), *Faith and Belief* (1979), and *Toward a World Theology* (1981). Smith's starting point reflects the many years he has spent comparing the experiences of religious believers from vastly different parts of the world. After looking at innumerable manifestations of religious faith in their historical development, Smith has been led to make a claim that is genuinely intriguing and daring at once. The human race has developed to a point where, today, we can begin to see that all the religious achievements of the human race are part of one common religious quest. History is one, Smith believes, because the religious story of the human race is one. "Those who believe in the unity of   humankind," writes Smith, "and those who believe in the unity of God, should be prepared therefore to discover the unity of humankind's religious history."[1] For millennia China has developed in considerably different ways from India. The tribal groups of the Amazon River basin have constructed their own cultural outlook with no contact with the Javanese. Religious dialogues between European Christians and Japanese Buddhists are very recent when measured by the calendar of world history. Today, however, what is obscured by sectarianism and simple ignorance—and also by academic overspecialization—is coming into focus: the unity of the entire human race in the universal religious quest for transcendence.

The gist of Smith's argument for a pluralist model of religions can be summarized as follows. First, at the core of all the religions is what Smith calls "faith." Religions provide their adherents with a sense of confidence or joy that comes from finding a meaning and purpose to life. Faith is the activity that puts a human being in touch with "transcendence," which is beyond all our many attempts to express with concepts. This is what Smith means by faith. Second, faith is universal. Every human being is capable of faith, and faith is made available to human beings through all of the religions of the world. Third, belief must be distinguished from faith. Beliefs differ from religion to religion and very often contradict one another. Even when they contradict one another, beliefs are expressions of the common faith that unifies the human religious quest. Fourth, Smith believes the world has developed to the point where we can now recognize the unity of all peoples in one common religious story based on the one faith expressed in the multitude of religious beliefs. Based on this common story, Smith calls for the creation of a "world theology" in which people of different religious traditions can begin to forge an understanding of one another and the one faith they all have in common. These four ideas need to be examined in greater detail.

The History of Religions in the Singular

Smith roots his hopes for a world theology in his belief in the universality of faith. Religious believers are obviously different. Some go on pilgrimage to Mecca, others to the Basilica of Our Lady of Guadalupe in Mexico. Some believers follow the Ten Commandments, others the Laws of Manu. Some religious believers offer sacrifices in cathedrals, others meditate before walls. For all their differences, Smith believes that all religious phenomena are expressions of a human activity that he calls "faith." Smith defines faith, to the extent that it can be defined at all, as

> ...a quiet confidence and joy which enables one to feel at home in the universe and to find meaning in the world and in one's life, a meaning which is profound and ultimate and is stable no matter what happens to oneself at the level of immediate event.[2]

Smith also is aware that his choice of terms has its limitations. In most forms of Buddhism, to give an obvious example, faith is not a prominent issue. The same is the case for Confucianism and Daoism. However, to the extent that all religious people can speak of "joy" in finding a home in the universe or "confidence" in discovering the meaning of life, Smith thinks the word *faith* can function as a suitable shorthand for the experience of transcendence.[3]

Second, Smith thinks of faith as "a universal quality of human life."[4] The Bedouin reciting the Qur'an, the Sioux dancing around the sacred hoop, the Zen monk in walking meditation, and the Guatemalan praying before the *Santos* are all expressions of this universal faith. In fact, Smith believes that the ability to open up to the transcendent is a basic human potency, present in every human being, even those who are not explicitly religious. Thus, the faith of Muslims and the faith of Christians are particular instances of a more general human capacity that can be seen in Buddhism and Hinduism and the other religions as well.

Third, faith must not to be confused with belief. Faith, which is a universal human quality, naturally needs to be expressed in one particular way or another. In this matter, human beings have shown no end of creativity across the millennia. Faith is expressed in the Noh dramas performed before Shinto shrines in Japan and the Passion Plays performed before Gothic cathedrals in Europe. Faith is also expressed in the architectures of the Shinto shrine and the Gothic cathedral. In addition, faith is expressed through religious beliefs. There is belief in the incarnation and the Holy Trinity among Christians and belief in the Four Noble Truths among Buddhists. Muslims believe that there is no God but God and that Muhammad is God's Prophet. Jews believe in the teachings of the Torah as God's law. For Smith, a religious belief is the expression of faith by means of a concept or idea.

> Belief, on the other hand, is the holding of certain ideas. Some might even see it as the intellect's translation (even reduction?) of transcendence into ostensible terms; the conceptualization in certain terms of the vision that, metaphorically, one has seen.[5]

To believe means to hold certain teachings to be true. Religious belief, therefore, is an activity of the mind made necessary by our need for clarifying and specifying our experience of faith. Religious belief, however, should never be equated with faith itself. Faith is deeper, more interior, and more personal than belief and has to do with the transcendent dimension of our lives as human beings.

Although Smith warns us that faith and belief are not to be confused, he nevertheless also recognizes that faith has no concrete existence apart from its manifold expressions in belief. Belief, along with religious art and ritual, makes faith tangible. Therefore, belief systems, or what Smith calls "theologies" even though not all religious believers use this term, are all responses to the one experience of the transcendent Smith calls faith. Throughout their long histories, the different religious traditions have been in a constant state of development. Each religion has had to construct a belief system in order to make sense of its experience of faith.

> All the various religious movements of the world, Christian and other, have been constructed, and have kept being constantly reconstructed and modified, by human beings—in response (in part) to something that transcends the movement and that they have recognized as transcending it.[6]

This means that the grand theological systems of beliefs, which are important aspects of the religions of the world, are human creations, not divinely ordained. Nevertheless, beliefs, such as the *Shahada* in Islam ("There is no God but God and Muhammad is God's Prophet) or the doctrine of no-self (*anatman*) in Buddhism, or belief in Amaterasu in Shinto, are not to be dismissed as *merely* human inventions.

> ...theologies may serve as channels introducing those who ponder them, and especially those who subscribe to them, those who see their significance, to a truth that in turn is more than human; more than finite; to God.[7]

As attempts to give concrete expression to the experience of the transcendent, all beliefs ultimately fail. But to think of them as complete failures would be a mistake. Thus, instead of saying, negatively, that beliefs are inadequate expressions of faith, more positively we should say that beliefs are more or less adequate in expressing the faith that they represent. Faith is mediated by religious belief.

The distinction between faith and belief is crucial to establishing Smith's vision of the unity of every human being in one single religious quest. The history of the many religions is in fact one history, one quest for the transcendent, because all human beings share in the one experience of the transcendent. Of course, the unity of the human race and its religious adventure are visible in faith, not belief. Judged in terms of their beliefs, human beings are very different. The Muslim's proclamation that "There is no God but God" can be contrasted with the Christian's belief in "Father, Son, and Holy Spirit." The Daoist's interest in the play of *yin* and *yang* is not the same as a Hindu's devotion to Krishna. Despite their obvious differences, all these beliefs are human expressions of the one human quest for transcendence. As believers, we are all different. As faith-filled human beings, we share in a common story.

This leads us to Smith's fourth basic point: the need for a "world theology."

83

A World Theology

Today we can recognize that the various histories of the many peoples of the world are but one history, the story of faith. The unity of our common religious quest has not been visible until the present era. Now, however, we are in a position to bring this invisible unity out into the open.[8] People of faith need to begin the process of reinterpreting their beliefs in the light of this common experience of faith. In effect, the era of Christian theology, as opposed to Islamic, Buddhist, Hindu, and other theology, has come to an end. What is needed now is a "world theology" in which the common experience of the transcendent will be expressed in beliefs embraced by all people of faith. Since in faith "our solidarity precedes our particularity,"[9] we now can become participants in the faith of others. One way to do this is by developing a global system of belief, a world theology.

The first task confronting us in the construction of a world theology is to recognize in the many different belief systems the underlying unity of faith. Currently, most Christians see Muslims as people who hold beliefs that are not true, according to Smith. Christians must come to look on Muslims as people of faith like themselves, but people who express their faith in ways which differ from the ways Christians express their faith. After we succeed in discerning the unity of faith amidst the diversity of beliefs, we will be in a position to begin to modify our own beliefs in keeping with the unity of faith. A world theology is a belief system in which people of faith around the world begin to conceptualize their one faith more consciously aware of the one history of faith that undergirds the separate histories of all the religions. The data for this world theology are the data that have accumulated from the study of all the different religions of the world. Smith's world theology will be truly nonsectarian—the world community of faith reflecting on the continuing story of its one faith.[10]

The purpose of Smith's world theology is not to perpetuate the beliefs that human beings have held until now. Neither is the purpose of this theology to blind ourselves to the truth of the beliefs human beings have cherished in the past. Rather, the purpose of a world theology is to understand past beliefs as expressions of the one faith that unites us all and then to reinterpret these beliefs in a way that contributes to our understanding of the one history of faith.

More precisely, how is this world theology to be done? A *Christian* theology of religions is unacceptably parochial to Smith. Exclusivist theologies, such as Karl Barth's, are obviously unacceptable to Smith. Inclusivist theologies, such as Karl Rahner's, are likewise unacceptable. Rahner's theology of the anonymous Christian is still based on the presupposition that Christianity's history of responding to the transcendent in faith is normative for everyone. Smith's world theology is meant to replace the parochial vision of Rahner's limited viewpoint. If speaking from within the Christian perspective on faith is unacceptably parochial, how then are Christians to make statements about their non-Christian neighbors?

On this score, Smith sets his sights very high. All people of faith must work toward a sympathetic understanding of their neighbors. In a world theology, no statement about a particular religion is valid if believers from that religion cannot agree with the statement.[11] In other words, in making claims about Buddhists or Daoists, a Christian must restrict her opinions to views that her Buddhist neighbor can recognize and accept. Smith believes that this highly restrictive standard for doing world theology is justified by the fact that if religious believers fail to recognize their faith in a statement we make about their religion, we are in fact still standing outside of their experience of faith as "nonparticipants." But since the lofty goal of Smith's world theology is to reflect together on our common experience of *faith*, not the many differences that exist in our beliefs, a Buddhist believer is justified in expecting to be able to recognize his faith when a Christian speaks about the Dharma. The reverse, of course, is also the case. Christians should be able to recognize their faith when Buddhists speak about the gospel.

Smith goes on to place an even higher burden on religious believers in regard to a world theology. No community of believers, such as Muslims, Jews, or Buddhists, should make a statement about themselves that someone from outside the community would reject. Here the requirements of Smith's world theology are demanding indeed. When Buddhists speak of themselves, they must make statements that Muslims and Jews, Hindus and Daoists, and all the other people of faith can accept. Of course this standard applies to Christians as well.

In order to comply with Smith's program, Christians will have to re-think in fundamental ways some of their most basic beliefs. In other words, in a world theology, a Christian must explain her belief that Jesus is the only-begotten Son of God in such a way that it does not contradict a Muslim's denial that Jesus is divine. But at the same time, a Muslim is not allowed to interpret Christianity's belief in the divinity of Jesus as idolatry, for the Muslim's Christian neighbor would not recognize herself in this interpretation of Christianity. Both the doctrines of the divinity of Jesus and the absolute Oneness of God are expressions of one human experience of faith.

Smith's requirements for a world theology, however, may not be as demanding as they might appear at first. The necessity of mutual agreement regarding different religious traditions applies only to faith, not to the actual religious beliefs themselves.

> At issue here is the momentous distinction between faith and belief, which I have felt it important to elaborate elsewhere. I personally tend to feel that there is probably no statement about my faith that I would wish to make that I could not on principle hope to explain to an intelligent, modern, devout, informed, Muslim or Hindu friend—and explain so that he would understand, and yes, in the end, would accept. Especially, I suppose, if he were something of a mystic, as well as a rationalist. Nor should I expect him to turn to "believe" anything, if he were intelligent, that I should not find both intelligible and intelligent. (What reason would he have for believing anything that I would not?)[12]

This passage leaves the reader unclear as to whether or not Muslims and Christians are allowed to disagree about the Qur'an as the final revelation of God as a belief, provided they do agree with one another regarding their common "faith." Christians must be in agreement with Muslims on the significance of this belief as an expression of the Muslim's faith, which according to Smith's definition, cannot be equated with the Muslim's belief. Apparently, however, "intelligent" Christians and Muslims, especially those who are "something of a rationalist and a mystic," would not believe anything that would lead to disagreements.[13]

One obvious conclusion to be drawn from this account of Smith's call for a world theology is that Christians will be required to revise their beliefs in significant ways. At the very least, Christians will be required to revise how they understand their beliefs. The doctrine of the incarnation cannot be a literal historical fact. Is it a "myth" (in John Hick's sense of the word)? Understanding the universal human quest for transcendence from within one religious perspective is not longer possible. The actual historical development of the different religious traditions has now advanced to the point where it is not possible to speak globally in a theology that is no longer merely Christian or Hindu, Muslim or Buddhist, but a world theology. Christians will have to expand their religious horizons considerably.[14]

Exclusivism, Inclusivism, and Idolatry

Smith's call for a world theology is yet another candidate for a pluralistic theology of religions. This means that, along with John Hick and Paul Knitter, Smith is a critic of exclusivist and inclusivist approaches to religious diversity. Christian statements about possessing the fullness of revelation in Jesus Christ or the necessity of faith in Jesus Christ for salvation are not acceptable in a world theology. In fact, exclusivist and inclusivist theologies can be seen as symptoms of what Smith calls "idolatry."

In the past, Christians have mistakenly claimed that non-Christians worship mere wood and stone. Christians have no monopoly on this problem. In fact, Smith locates the origin of this mistake in Christianity's roots in Judaism.[15] *Idolatry* is a word used to denigrate and dismiss another's religious commitments by refusing to recognize that there is a genuine faith present in the religious life of someone from outside one's own religious tradition. Smith's thesis is that,

> all of us on earth are prone to an error, one that Western theology, unfortunately, has tended at times to bless: the error of identifying with the divine, with the truth, with the final, with transcendence, the particular form in or through which we have been introduced to it....[16]

There is a great irony at work here that Smith seeks to underscore. Those who naively identify their own beliefs with the absolute and final truth are the first to accuse others of idol worship. The irony lies in the fact that the one who has made his or her beliefs absolute is the one guilty of idolatry. By naively equating our own belief system with the absolute truth, mere belief becomes a substitute for faith, an idol that obscures the experience of faith.

From the perspective of a world theology, according to Smith, Christians should not say that God has been revealed only in Jesus Christ, for there are revelations of God outside of Christianity.[17] Neither is it proper to say that God is revealed fully and definitively in Jesus Christ alone. Ironically, by placing so much emphasis on the unparalleled uniqueness of Jesus, Christians risk losing sight of the transcendent God who is revealed through Jesus. God saves human beings. To think that only Christianity is true or salvific is to have lost faith in the God that lies beyond Christianity. Exclusivism and inclusivism are forms of idolatry.

What about the often-heard claim that Christianity is based on a supernatural revelation from God? When this supernatural revelation is restricted to Christianity, we are led inevitably to Barth's exclusivist theology of religions. When this supernatural revelation is present implicitly in other religions, we are led to Rahner's inclusivist theology of the "anonymous Christian." Smith responds to this issue by noting that the idea of a supernatural revelation is a belief as well. That is to say, belief in the notion of a supernatural revelation from God is one way to conceptualize the experience of faith. As a belief, this notion also is a human response to the transcendent that needs to be reinterpreted today in light of our one religious history. As a belief, this notion is only more or less adequate as an interpretation of the experience of faith. To the extent that this belief leads to exclusivist or inclusivist attitudes toward other religions, the idea of a supernatural revelation is not adequate to our awareness of faith today and the demands of a truly world theology.[18]

Running through all the many religions of the world is a common human experience of the transcendent. Religious beliefs, even beliefs that contradict each other, are expressions of this transcendent reality. We now know enough about one another to recognize this fact and to begin to think about our one experience of faith together. According to Smith, the various religious traditions of the world have developed to the point where it is now possible for us to move beyond the sectarian thinking and begin to develop a world theology. Here lies the historical starting point for Smith's pluralistic understanding of religious diversity.

Stanley Samartha

The last of the pluralists we shall discuss is noteworthy because he was born and raised in India and his approach to the entire question of a pluralistic theology of religions has been thoroughly shaped by what he calls the traditional religious pluralism of his homeland. In addition to his South Asian background, Stanley Samartha served for many years as the first director of the Dialogue Program of the World Council of Churches. As an Indian, he was born into a culture of immense religious diversity, and as a Christian theologian he has struggled with the meaning of that diversity for some time. In addition to numerous journal articles and public addresses, he is the author of books such as *The Hindu Response to the Unbound Christ, One Christ—Many Religions*, and *Courage for Dialogue: Ecumenical Issues in Interreligious Relationships*.[19]

Samartha's Indian perspective on pluralism has emerged gradually in his work. Early on, his writings reflected the official positions taken by the World Council of Churches. For years, the official position of the WCC was indebted in no small way to the exclusivist outlook of Karl Barth.[20] Starting around 1966, this exclusivist view began to give way to a more inclusivist point of view. The God of Jesus Christ has called Christians into dialogue with peoples of other faiths and ideologies.[21] The light of God is revealed through all religions, but normatively and fully only in Jesus Christ.[22] Later, Samartha became a critic of this inclusivist approach and began to integrate the immense religious legacy of his native India with his understanding of Christianity.[23] Not surprisingly, one theme in Samartha's work that has been especially controversial has been the problem of the uniqueness of Christ. Seen from within the perspective of India's traditionally pluralistic approach to religious diversity, Christ must be seen as one savior among many. In India, Christians will have to deal with this fact in depth.[24]

What God Has Relativized

Along with other voices calling for a pluralistic theology of religions, Stanley Samartha is concerned that the official calls for interreligious dialogue by the Catholic Church and the World Council of Churches have stalled over the problem of Christianity's missionary impulse. One important way to get the Christian churches back on track is to call into question Christianity's exclusivist and inclusivist claims in light of our multireligious situation. This means facing the issue of the incarnation squarely.

According to Samartha, the doctrine of the incarnation means that God, by entering into the world at a particular time and place, has freely chosen to become relative within history. By coming into the world in the form of a human being, the absolute God has become subject to the limitations of time and space, of culture and language. In Jesus, God has revealed himself in the form of a first-century Palestinian Jew. This does not imply, however, that there is anything absolute about Jesus' early Jewish mentality, or the language that he spoke, or the historical circumstances within which he taught. From this Samartha draws a demanding conclusion. When speaking of Jesus Christ, "Christian theologians should...ask themselves whether they are justified in absolutizing in doctrine him whom God has relativized in history."[25]

In effect, Samartha is reflecting on the particularity of Jesus by taking it in a very nontraditional direction. Karl Barth looks on the incarnation in terms of the "scandal of particularity": God has chosen a specific time and place within the world; indeed, God has chosen a specific individual from among all the human beings who have ever lived and has given that human being a centrality and a unique meaning that are now normative for all human beings. As God chose the Jews and not the Egyptians to be his people in the story of the exodus, so also God has chosen Jesus, and not Vishnu or Confucius or Siddhartha Gautama, to be his Son. For Barth, God is not known in a general revelation to all, but only by means of a special revelation at a particular historical time and place and in a particular human being. This is Barth. Samartha interprets the life and death of Jesus of Nazareth in a significantly different way. In Jesus, Christians must recognize the fact that God has become "relative." God can be revealed within the world in any number of partial and limited ways. Therefore, what God has made relative in history, theologians must not make absolute in doctrine. Jesus is not the unique and final revelation of God. The "particularity" of Jesus, as a first-century Palestinian Jew, is not a scandal at all, but rather just another example of God being revealed in the world in a limited and finite way.

The point of Samartha's nonnormative understanding of the incarnation is to equip Christians for living better with the fact of religious diversity. Older, more traditional views of Jesus Christ, which form the basis of exclusivist and inclusivist theologies of religions, must give way to what Samartha calls the "relational distinctiveness" of Jesus Christ.[26] Our understanding of Jesus must be "relational" because what God has done for the world in Jesus is related to what God has done for the world through the other faiths. Simultaneously, our understanding of Jesus must be "distinctive" because God has revealed himself in the many religions in distinctive ways. Recognizing the "relational distinctiveness" of Jesus as one of the revelations of God to the world will help to move Christians away from an exclusivist view of non-Christian religions and the missionary impulse to convert non-Christians and toward more of an appreciation of what it is about these religions that holds such a profound grasp on the imagination of their adherents.

As we saw in the work of John Hick and Paul Knitter, Samartha's call for a pluralistic theology of religions carries with it major repercussions for our understanding of Jesus Christ as the one, unique, and final savior of the world.

> That Jesus is the Christ of God is a confession of faith by the Christian community. It does indeed remain normative to Christians everywhere, but to make it "absolutely singular" and to maintain that the meaning of the Mystery is disclosed only in one particular person at one particular point, and nowhere else, is to ignore one's neighbors of other faiths who have other points of reference.[27]

This is not to say that there is nothing distinctive about Jesus, only that the distinctiveness of Jesus cannot be understood in ways that lead to an exclusivist understanding of Christianity in relation to the other religions of the world.

But on the issue of Jesus' distinctiveness, Samartha, seemingly, is willing to let go more of the Christian tradition than even John Hick. In keeping with his notion of the incarnation as a "myth," that is, language that is not to be taken literally, presumably Hick thinks Christians can continue to make statements such as, "Jesus Christ is God." The point is that statements such as these are not to be taken literally. Samartha apparently thinks that statements such as this are not admissible even as nonliteral, or "mythological" statements.

> The distinctiveness of Jesus Christ does not lie in claiming that "Jesus Christ is God." This amounts to saying that Jesus Christ is the tribal god of Christians over against the gods of other peoples. Elevating Jesus to the status of God or limiting Christ to Jesus of Nazareth are both temptations to be avoided.[28]

Traditionally, Christians have used metaphysics to understand how Jesus is divine. In the words of the Nicene Creed, Jesus Christ is "one in being with the Father." Samartha argues that this metaphysical understanding of Jesus' divinity makes dialogue with other religions impossible.[29] Understanding Jesus as "relationally distinct" allows Christians to shift their attention from a defensive view of Jesus' divinity to a focus on Jesus' preaching of God and his kingdom. This will allow Christians to remain committed to Jesus without having to disparage other religions in order to do so.

Pluralism in the Indian Tradition

Samartha's call for a new understanding of Jesus Christ has much in common with the pluralistic theologies of John Hick and Paul Knitter. As a pluralist theologian, however, Samartha has the right to claim his own distinctiveness. I refer to his interest in founding his pluralistic theology of religions on the legacy of the religious pluralism of his South Asian homeland, India.

In India, harmony among religions is far more than an academic question. What religions say about themselves and about each other has political and social ramifications.[30] Reflecting on the problem of religiously oriented violence in India, Samartha underscores the *political* consequences that result when religions make exclusivist claims. Traditionally, religions in India have been sources of social renewal and cultural creativity. Now they are increasingly being criticized as causes of social unrest. A pluralistic theology of religions can contribute to the healing that needs to go on. For religions in India, the adoption of a pluralistic theology of religions represents a *return* to an ancient tradition.

This ancient tradition can be traced back to the Rig Veda, among the very oldest of religious texts in India's long history. In the Rig Veda, we are told that Truth (*Sat*) is One even though sages call it by different names. In addition, the One is greater than all the gods.[31] The Rig Veda, moreover, is only the beginning of a long tradition of pluralism. In India, worship of any particular god has long been considered the worship of the transcendent One.[32] Even in the great Hindu devotional systems, such as the worship of Vishnu, the central deity was often recognized as the personal face of the transcendent unity that lies at the foundation of all reality.

To locate the theological foundations for India's indigenous brand of religious pluralism, Samartha looks to India's religious history. Two principles have generally governed the relationships between religions in India. First, from ancient times Indian theologians have spoken of the unity (*mataikya*) of all religions. Second, they have tried to show that religions, properly understood, do not contradict one another (*matavirodha*). From these two principles, Indian theologians have often concluded that the plurality of religions is natural and inevitable, an expression of *Dharma* (truth, the nature of things) and a reflection of the diversity of human temperaments. To assert otherwise only breeds violence. In this respect, religious diversity can be related to the law of karma. There are many religions because human beings are born with differing aptitudes and preferences that make one religious path more suitable and helpful than another. In effect, our karma makes some of us more suited to devotionalism and others more adept at mysticism or asceticism. Hindus are not Christians, in this view of religious diversity, because of their karma. For a Hindu to become a Christian would be to try to change one's karma.[33]

India's traditional pluralism, however, has always been set in a very delicate balance. This balance was upset by the arrival of Islam under the Moguls and Christianity under the British.

> Islam and later Christianity, armed with their exclusive claims and allied with military, political, and economic power, rudely intruded into India's delicate balance of relationships. This created deep disturbances within Indian consciousness, the consequences of which are with us even to this day.[34]

This traditional Indian view of religious diversity forms the basis of a critique of Christianity's claims to superiority over other religions. Hinduism's rejection of Christianity's exclusivism, Samartha reminds us, arises not only because this outlook is foreign to India's cultural and religious tradition but also because Christian exclusivism is politically destabilizing.

> In no other country, therefore, does the claim for the "uniqueness" of one particular religious tradition or the assertion of the "normativeness" of one particular faith over others sound so rude, out of place, and theologically arrogant as in India. Such assertions contradict India's whole ethos and tear at the fabric of interreligious relationships so carefully woven during centuries of conflict, tension, and massive sufferings by the people.[35]

The implications of India's traditional pluralism for Christianity's missionary effort are massive, and Samartha does not hold back in making these implications explicit.

> Therefore the question of superiority or "uniqueness" of any one Dharma [religion/teaching] over others does not arise. Criticism of one religion based on criteria derived from another is unwarranted. Conversions are unnecessary. The Hindus are not asking Christians to give up their commitment to God in Christ. Rather, they are pleading with Christians not to ask Hindus to give up their commitment.[36]

Samartha concludes that missionary activity by Christians in India is not proper, if that missionary activity is understood as the effort to bap-

tize Hindus or Muslims into the Christian fold. Instead the mission of
the church in India must be one of service to the poor.

> God's creative and recreative activity provides the larger source
> from which streams of God's revealing and saving activity flow
> into the river of history. This creative and redeeming activity of
> God is prior to and more comprehensive than the church's mis-
> sion, and directs our attention beyond the church to the Kingdom.
> This has nothing to do with the expansion of Christianity as a re-
> ligion or the statistical increase of Christians in the world.[37]

In India, it would seem, Hinduism is an instrument of God's saving activity. The numerical increase of Christians does much to destabilize Indian
society, but contributes nothing new to the salvation of that ancient land.

India Instructs Christianity

Reflecting the traditions of his homeland in South Asia, Samartha
believes we can come to a new understanding of how the many religions might live peaceably with one another, an understanding that is
compatible with Christianity and is also deeply informed by the traditional religious pluralism of India. In regard to our need for a theology of religions, how might India instruct Christianity? So far Samartha
has mentioned the unity of religions (*mataikya*) and the belief that ultimately religions do not contradict one another (*matavirodha*).
Christians can use both of these principles in developing a pluralistic
theology of religions that is relevant to the complexities of the day. The
unity of all the religions arises out of an affirmation of the oneness of
all in a transcendent Mystery. The freedom that the different religions
enjoy from contradicting each other requires Christians to abandon
their exclusivist claims.

When Samartha locates the unity of all religions in a transcendent
Mystery, he is not suggesting that we suffer from a confusion or lack of
knowledge. The Mystery to which all religions point is a matter of intuition, not analysis. The Mystery beyond all the religions is "near yet far,
knowable yet unknowable, intimate yet ultimate."[38] In Samartha's view,
Mystery is "the Truth of the Truth" and "the transcendent Center that

remains always beyond and greater than apprehensions of it or even the sum total of those apprehensions."[39] In Samartha's estimation, Mystery indicates that diversity is within the heart of Being itself and therefore may be intrinsic to human nature as well.[40] In fact, the Mystery that lies beyond all our understandings of it is what makes pluralism possible.[41] At the same time, this affirmation of one, transcendent Mystery beyond all the religions should not be taken as an excuse for dodging our responsibility for rational inquiry into the truth of religious questions. The transcendent Mystery, however, does pose a critique of logic and concepts as the only way to do theology. Where the philosopher and theologian lose the trail, the mystic continues to ascend the mount.

Samartha's notion of Mystery has much in common with what John Hick calls "the Real," what Paul Knitter calls *sótéria*, and what Wilfred Cantwell Smith calls "the transcendent." All three are absolutes that lie beyond the various religions; yet all can be expressed in religious beliefs. No particular expression of the transcendent absolute can be held up as normative. In addition, Samartha's Mystery would seem to have much in common with Karl Rahner's notion of the Holy Mystery, which provides the basis for his inclusivist theology of religions. In formulating his inclusivist theology, Rahner appealed to the notion of a transcendent Mystery. But the similarity between the two Christian theologians is superficial. Samartha and Rahner are in agreement that responses to Mystery are legion, as manifold as the many religions of the earth. But unlike Rahner, Samartha does not believe that any particular religious response to Mystery can be separated out from the pack as superior, unique, or normative for the rest.

> The history of religions shows that these responses are many and are different, sometimes even within a particular religious tradition. Quite often these differences are due to cultural and historical factors. Although each response to Mystery has a normative claim on the followers of that particular tradition, the criteria derived for one response cannot be made the norm to judge the responses of other traditions.[42]

Two obviously pertinent examples would be the Hindu doctrine of Brahman and the Christian doctrine of God.[43] For Samartha, both are responses to the one, transcendent Mystery that lies beyond Hinduism and Christianity. Both concepts are the result of different historical and cultural conditions. As theological concepts, both God and Brahman are but pale reflections of the Mystery they attempt to express in words. That being the case, neither of the two terms can be used as a norm to judge the other. God is not closer to hitting the mark than Brahman or vice versa. Instead, the two terms "can only be symbolic, pointing to the Mystery."[44]

The first of the two principles Samartha has taken from the Indian tradition has to do with the ultimate unity of all religions (*mataikya*). Christians should accept this unity using the notion of a transcendent Mystery. The second principle has to do with the traditional Indian belief that religions do not really contradict each other (*matavirodha*). By integrating this second principle into their understanding of themselves, Christians will come to realize the necessity to reject exclusivism.[45]

Exclusivist theologies put fences around Mystery. They pretend to place limitations on what cannot be limited. In exclusivist claims, rational propositions eclipse the mystical. Worst of all, in a place like India, exclusivism separates Christians from the community of religious faiths.[46] Instead of exclusivism, Christians need to come to a better understanding of their own distinctiveness as a religious community, but in relation to the other religions. This agenda for Christians stems from Samartha's earlier appeal to understand Jesus in terms of his "relational distinctiveness." No religion is quite like Christianity. This recognition of uniqueness, however, applies equally to every other religion as well. No religion is quite like Sikhism, Buddhism, Islam, Jainism, or Hinduism either. All religions are distinct, but intimately related. In understanding itself in terms of a "relational distinctiveness," Christians in India will have adopted a way of understanding themselves that is a time-honored tradition in that part of the world.[47]

A Christian theology of religions, inspired by the traditional pluralism of India will be theocentric. God, the "Mysterious Other" who lies beyond all its many manifestations, is the basis for the unity and cooperation of all the religions. As the Other that defies all our attempts to domesticate it in theological concepts and religious doctrines, the divine Mystery makes every religion relative to every other religion. Nor do

Christians need to regret the relativity of all the religions, including their own. The recognition that Christianity is not the absolute truth itself is a kind of religious experience of the divine Mystery that encompasses all and includes all the religions.

> The Other relativizes everything else. In fact, the willingness to accept such relativization is perhaps the only real guarantee that one has encountered the Other as ultimately real.[48]

Christians theologians should not make absolute what God has made relative. By revealing himself within history in the life and preaching of Jesus of Nazareth, the divine Mystery has become as limited and nonabsolute as every other human being. The revelation of Mystery in Jesus is distinct but not absolute, and Christians need to recognize this truth about their religion. This is one of the first points Samartha makes.

Therefore, Christians must change the way they talk about their faith in Jesus. If the great religious traditions of the world are in fact "different responses to the one Mystery of God or *Sat* or the Transcendent or Ultimate Reality," then Christians must ensure that their account of the distinctiveness of their own religion is stated "in such a way that a mutually critical and enriching *relationship* between different responses becomes naturally possible."[49] Exclusivism is a form of theological imperialism, the attempt to conquer other faiths. Inclusivism, exclusivism's "patronizing cousin," attempts to co-opt our religious neighbors. Both are forms of theological violence that, in India at least, can be connected with social violence. In regard to Christianity's need for a pluralistic theology of religions, Christians have much to learn from India.

*   *   *

In order to be adequate for the needs of Christians today, a theology of religions must be responsible to the demands of the Christian tradition and at the same time assist Christians in responding creatively to the opportunity religious diversity offers us today. In the last three chapters, I have summarized the pluralist proposals of John Hick, Paul Knitter, Wilfred Cantwell Smith, and Stanley Samartha with

98

very little criticism of their positions. How do the pluralists measure up to the two criteria for an adequate theology of religions? Are the various candidates for a pluralist theology in keeping with Christian tradition? Do these pluralistic models of religious diversity encourage Christians to look on their non-Christian neighbors with respect and humility? The next two chapters offer a discussion of the failures of the pluralists.

NOTES

1. Wilfred Cantwell Smith, *Toward a World Theology* (Philadelphia: Westminster Press), 4.

2. Wilfred Cantwell Smith, *Faith and Belief* (Princeton: Princeton University Press, 1979), 12.

3. Ibid., 3–9. See also idem, *Toward a World Theology*, 47–49.

4. Smith, *Toward a World Theology*, 113–18.

5. Smith, *Faith and Belief*, 12.

6. Wilfred Cantwell Smith, "Idolatry in Comparative Perspective," in *The Myth of Christian Uniqueness: Toward a Pluralistic Theology of Religions*, ed. John Hick and Paul Knitter (Maryknoll, N.Y.: Orbis Books, 1987), 59.

7. Ibid., 56.

8. Smith, *Toward a World Theology*, 37–44.

9. Ibid., 103.

10. Ibid., 108.

11. Ibid., 97–102.

12. Ibid., 101–2.

13. Ibid., 97.

14. Smith, *Faith and Belief*, 156.

15. See Smith, "Idolatry in Comparative Perspective," 54–55.

16. Ibid., 58–59.

17. Smith, *Toward a World Theology*, 175.

18. Smith, *Faith and Belief*, 69.

19. Stanley J. Samartha, *The Hindu Response to the Unbound Christ* (Bangalore: Christian Institute for the Study of Religion and Society, 1974); idem, *One Christ—Many Religions: Toward a Revised Christology* (Maryknoll, N.Y.: Orbis Books, 1991); idem, *Courage for Dialogue: Ecumenical Issues in Interreligious Relationships* (Maryknoll, N.Y.: Orbis Books, 1982), 151–52. For a collection of essays devoted to Samartha's contribution to the question of religious diversity, see *Dialogue in Community: Essays in Honor of Stanley J. Samartha*, ed. Constantine Jathana (Mangalore, India: Karnataka Theological Research Institute, 1982).

20. Barth's influence on the World Council of Churches was exerted through the leadership of Hendrick Kraemer, at least until 1966. For Kraemer's views of religious diversity and its Barthian overtones, see Hendrick Kraemer, *The Christian Message in a Non-Christian World* (London: Harper & Brothers, 1938).

21. Stanley J. Samartha, "Dialogue as a Continuing Christian

Concern," in *Living Faiths and the Ecumenical Movement*, ed. S. J. Samartha (Geneva: WCC, 1971), reprinted in *Christianity and the Other Religions*, ed. John Hick and Brian Hebblethwaite (Philadelphia: Fortress Press, 1980), 151–70.

22. Samartha, *Hindu Response*.

23. Stanley J. Samartha, "The Lordship of Jesus Christ and Religious Pluralism," in *Christ's Lordship and Religious Pluralism*, ed. Gerald H. Anderson and Thomas F. Stransky, C.S.P. (Maryknoll, N.Y.: Orbis Books, 1981), 19-36.

24. For Samartha's reflections on the need to ground an understanding of Christ in the Indian religious tradition, see *One Christ—Many Religions*, 92–131.

25. Stanley J. Samartha, "The Cross and the Rainbow: Christ in a Multi-religious Culture," in *The Myth of Christian Uniqueness: Toward a Pluralistic Theology of Religions*, ed. John Hick and Paul Knitter (Maryknoll, N.Y.: Orbis Books, 1987), 69.

26. Ibid., 70.

27. Ibid., 76.

28. Ibid., 79.

29. Ibid., 80.

30. Samartha, *One Christ—Many Religions*, 45–57. See also Samartha, "The Cross and the Rainbow," 72.

31. Samartha, "The Cross and the Rainbow," 73.

32. See Samartha, *One Christ—Many Religions*, 80–81.

33. Ibid., 81.

34. Samartha, "The Cross and the Rainbow," 73–74. Among India's multiple responses to British colonialism and the "intrusion" of Christianity into the Indian subcontinent was a Hindu revival movement championed by figures such as Ram Mohan Roy (1772–1833) and S. Radhakrishnan (1888–1975). These early figures in the "neo-Hinduism" movement argued against Christian claims to superiority by appealing to a pluralistic understanding of religions based on versions of India's *Advaita Vedanta* philosophy. Samartha thinks of this movement as more of a political statement than a theological statement.

35. Samartha, "The Cross and the Rainbow," 75.

36. Ibid., 74.

37. Samartha, *One Christ—Many Religions*, 150.

38. Samartha, "The Cross and the Rainbow," 75.

39. Ibid.

40. Ibid.

41. Samartha, *One Christ—Many Religions*, 80.
42. Samartha, "The Cross and the Rainbow," 76.
43. Ibid.
44. Ibid.
45. Ibid., 77.
46. Samartha, *One Christ—Many Religions*, 98–103.
47. Samartha, "The Cross and the Rainbow," 81.
48. Samartha, *Courage for Dialogue*, 151–52.
49. Samartha, "The Cross and the Rainbow," 79.

Chapter 5

HOW HELPFUL IS PLURALISM?

Exclusivism and pluralism take positions on the meaning of religious diversity that hug opposite shores. Both cannot be true, but both can be false.[1] In the first chapter, we noted that exclusivist theories, like Barth's, run afoul of the two criteria we have held up for an adequate Christian response to the fact of religious diversity: (1) faithfulness to the Christian tradition and (2) helpfulness in assisting Christians to respond creatively to religious diversity. The present chapter looks at some of the major criticisms that have been mounted against the pluralists using these same criteria. The discussion in this present chapter will be limited to problems with the pluralist proposals of John Hick, Wilfred Cantwell Smith, and Stanley Samartha. The following chapter will look at the work of Paul Knitter.

John Hick has called for a Copernican revolution within Christianity, where "the Real" and not Christ is given pride of place at the center of the universe of faiths. Wilfred Cantwell Smith bases his hopes for a "world theology" on a distinction between our common faith and our differing beliefs. Stanley Samartha sees the unity of all religions in a transcendent Mystery that lies beyond them all. Now the critics of these views will have an opportunity to be heard.[2] To the extent that the proposals of the pluralists share common elements, there are common themes to be found in the voices of their critics. For example, pluralists often assert that all religions are responses to or expressions of a transcendent Absolute (the Real, the transcendent, Mystery), or that religions share in a common religious experience (faith). Linked to this assertion

103

is the pluralist's fondness for drawing a clear line between what can be known and what is utterly beyond our knowing. A third element common to the pluralists is their general agreement that Christians will have to abandon or at least reinterpret their traditional belief in Jesus Christ as the unique savior of the world. Not surprisingly, criticisms of the pluralist program for responding to religious diversity have clustered around these themes. Since Paul Knitter's work represents the most highly developed argument against the traditional belief in Jesus Christ as unique savior of the world, we will come to this issue in the chapter that follows. For now, the first two common themes will hold our attention.

Today the diversity of religions poses a challenge to Christians but also offers them an opportunity of incomparable value. When Christians take their non-Christian neighbors seriously, when they recognize in their neighbors not only similarity but also genuinely significant differences in their deepest-held religious convictions, Christians believers will not be left untouched. The depth and richness Christians find in the religious lives of their non-Christian neighbors can be threatening. By taking non-Christian religions seriously, Christians may feel the anxiety that comes from realizing that their religion is but one among many. The religious traditions of our non-Christian neighbors enable them to lead full and humane lives quite apart from faith in Jesus Christ. Encounters with their non-Christian neighbors, on the other hand, can also be an opportunity for Christians to learn much of value and to return to their own religious tradition with new insight. This is what I mean by a "creative response to religious diversity."

Does the pluralist program equip Christians to respond to the threat and the opportunity of religious diversity today? In light of this challenge, exclusivist and inclusivist approaches to religious diversity have been found wanting. Pluralist theories should be measured by the same standards.

Pluralism: Really a "Hypothesis"?

In one of his early works, John Hick tells the Indian folktale of the elephant and the six blind men. An elephant is brought before six blind men who begin to touch different parts of the elephant. The one who feels the trunk believes that an elephant is like a snake. The one who feels the ear believes that an elephant is like a great banana leaf. The one who feels the feet believes an elephant is like a tree trunk. In his early work, Hick took this folktale as a natural parable for his understanding of religious pluralism: all the religions of the world have a partial understanding of a transcendent Reality that is far greater than any one religious tradition knows. All the religions are partial and incomplete interpretations of a transcendent Absolute.[3]

Hick's critics have tried to hoist him on his own petard. By appealing to the story of the elephant and the six blind men, Hick would seem to imply that he is the only one among us who is not blind. The different religious traditions each have their own, very limited, view of the truth, which apparently blinds religious believers to the whole picture. John Hick, in contrast, sees what other religious believers cannot see. Hick bristles at this criticism of his position.[4] The question, however, remains: How do pluralists know that all the religions are but partial truths? Hick seems to be claiming to know what most traditional religious believers do not know, namely, that all religions have "reality-centeredness" in common.

Hick has tried to dodge this bullet by claiming that his pluralist theory is a *hypothesis* only.[5] One of his most succinct statements of this hypothesis can be found in *An Interpretation of Religion*. The diversity of religious phenomena have been interpreted variously in the modern world. Skepticism holds that all religions are wrong. Dogmatism (in both its exclusivist and inclusivist forms) maintains that all religions are wrong with the exception of one's own religion. Hick seeks to promote a third alternative, the pluralist position, in which one's own religion is true and other religions are true as well.

> ...the great...faiths constitute different ways of experiencing, conceiving and living in relation to an ultimate divine Reality which transcends all our varied visions of it.[6]

This claim, however, is not a simple assertion, for this would be as dogmatic as exclusivism and inclusivism. Rather, the claim should be taken as a hypothesis only. Adopting this hypothesis will allow believers from different religious traditions to live harmoniously with one another.

Taking the pluralist position as a hypothesis is also a way for John

Hick to respond to the charge of omniscience. Pluralism is merely a hypothesis, not a pronouncement from on high by one who claims to see what other religious believers cannot see. Like any good hypothesis, the pluralist hypothesis is built inductively from experience. After looking at the many teachings of the world's different faiths, the idea that all religions are reflections of one transcendent Absolute is the most sensible theory to account for all the data. Pluralism, therefore, should be taken as a practical suggestion, a working presupposition for dealing with religious diversity with tolerance and openness. The theory should not be taken as a simple assertion about all the religions, but rather as an appropriate way to make sense out of the facts, a better way than skepticism and dogmatism.

Is Hick's pluralist theory really a hypothesis? I do not believe it is. In order to be a hypothesis, there must exist conditions under which the pluralist position might be proved wrong. If there is no way for a hypothesis to be disproved, it cannot rightly be considered a hypothesis at all. Rather it is simply a raw assertion. For example, in physics, in order to explain how light waves moved across space, physicists developed the "ether" hypothesis. "Ether" was thought to be the all-pervasive stuff through which light waves pass. As ocean waves need water in order to travel through the sea, so also light waves need a medium. Without a medium to pass through, no wave phenomenon makes sense. In 1887, Albert A. Michaelson and Edward W. Morely performed the famous experiment with their interferometer that showed that the "ether" does not exist. The ether really was a hypothesis in the proper sense: as a theory to make sense out of the observed facts, it could be proved wrong. A hypothesis based on Einstein's theory of relativity held that light would be bent when passing near a massive gravitational field. Einstein's prediction was a real hypothesis as well because it could be put to the test by observing light coming to earth from the planet Mercury during an eclipse of the sun. This hypothesis stands to this day. Here again, we have a real hypothesis because the possibility exists for proving it wrong.

John Hick claims to have a hypothesis as well. For example, Christians believe in a God who is both transcendent and also active within human history in the person of Jesus Christ. Vaishnavite Hindus believe that Vishnu, their supreme divinity, has appeared among human beings as Krishna. According to Hick's hypothesis, both Christianity's

God and Lord Vishnu should be taken as differing interpretations of the same Ultimate Reality. If pluralism is really a hypothesis, we may rightly ask John Hick to specify under which conditions the hypothesis could be proved wrong. One possibility would be to point out that Daoists speak of the Dao instead of appealing to a personal divinity like Christianity and Hinduism. The Dao is not a transcendent Creator, nor has it entered into history in human form, like Jesus. The Dao is not a person to whom a devotee might pray. Instead, Daoists speak of the Dao in terms of the dynamic interplay of *yin* and *yang* unfolding everywhere. Here it would seem that we have a real difference between religions. Christians think of their God as the Holy One who saved his chosen people from the slavery of Egypt and gave them the Promised Land, who raised up the prophets to call his people back to fidelity to the covenant and eventually sent the world his only Son to be our redeemer. The Dao, on the other hand, has not entered into history to save his chosen people, nor is the Dao a redeemer as Jesus is for Christians.

Does this significant difference separating Daoism and Christianity prove John Hick's hypothesis wrong? Apparently it does not, because, like T'ien in Confucianism and the Buddha Nature in Mahayana Buddhism, the Dao is but another example of the *impersonal* manifestations of the Real which complement all the *personal* manifestations of it such as Jesus, Krishna, Allah, and for that matter, Amaterasu, Aphrodite, and Kali.[7] In fact, what could we possibly discover about the many religions of the world that would suggest that Hick's "hypothesis" is in fact a mistake? There seems to be no actual fact about the religions of the world that Hick cannot immediately cover with the umbrella of his transcendental Absolute. John Hick might be right about the transcendental unity of all the religions. But even if he is correct, pluralism is still not a hypothesis. If no objection can be raised to prove the pluralist hypothesis wrong, what we have is a religious assertion and not a hypothesis at all.[8]

In my view, pluralism is a rather implausible assertion made in the face of a vast amount of concrete data suggesting the contrary. When Christians talk about a creator God who has entered into the history of the world in the life and death of Jesus Christ, they certainly seem to be referring to something that differs in really basic ways from what Daoists mean when they speak about the *Dao* as the infinite interplay of *yin* and *yang*, or what Muslims mean when they speak of Muhammad as

God's last and greatest Prophet. To believe otherwise, even for the best of intentions, requires us to ignore basic facts about the different religious traditions and the claims religious believers make about themselves. Of course there are real similarities that link religions to one another, and these should not be denied. However, to assume from the start that all religions are responses to a common, transcendent Absolute that is beyond all possible characterization is to dismiss the real differences that distinguish religions from one another.

Hick tries to save his "hypothesis" by giving it a major epicycle, his notion of "eschatological verification," or the idea that the pluralist thesis can be proved correct or in error only after death in the world to come.[9] In taking this approach, Hick concedes that there is no way that pluralism could possibly be proved wrong in this life. However, after death, or after the end of the world (i.e., "eschatologically"), the pluralist thesis can be proved wrong; therefore, it is truly a hypothesis.[10] This argument seems especially slippery to a critic like S. Mark Heim. If the transcendent Absolute behind all the religions can never be known as it is in itself, as Hick maintains, then when a Christian dies and enters into the Beatific Vision, does this mean that Buddhists were wrong all along about Nirvana? Hick's belief in the unknowability of the Absolute allows us to believe that the Beatific Vision is merely the Christian interpretation of what Buddhists call Nirvana. Pluralists are still not required to change their mind about religious diversity, even dead pluralists.[11] This last point leads us to some of the implications of the fact that pluralism is not a hypothesis but a religious assertion.

Knowing More Than Other People

Pluralism is an assertion about the way religions really are and not a hypothesis open to being confirmed or disproved. What difference does this make? Major repercussions flow from the fact that the pluralist position is not a hypothesis, including significant repercussions for Christians interested in responding creatively to religious diversity. Here I want to address two issues specifically. First, Christians who adopt the pluralist model place themselves in a difficult position. As pluralists, these Christians claim to know more about other religious believers than these believers know about themselves. Second, Christians who adopt the pluralist position never have to change their minds. This is because the pluralists establish their view of the many religions in such a way that no concrete fact can be offered that would indicate that the pluralist position in fact is not the case. Both of these problems indicate that pluralism will not be helpful for Christians interested in responding creatively to their non-Christian neighbors.

The first issue has to do with what pluralists know about religious believers from faiths other than their own. Pluralists like John Hick have criticized inclusivists such as Karl Rahner. As a Christian inclusivist, Rahner believes that the same saving grace of Jesus Christ, which Christians see at work in their own lives, is also at work in the lives of non-Christians. For this reason, Christians are obliged to look upon non-Christians as "Christians without the name" or "anonymous Christians." In Hick's view, the inclusivist approach places Christians in the intolerable position of claiming to know more about the religious lives of Buddhists or Muslims than they know themselves. Despite what non-Christians might believe, it is really Christ who saves them through the symbols, liturgies and tenets of their religion. Inclusivism, therefore, must be counted as arrogance, a way for Christians to excuse themselves from having to take non-Christians seriously and a great hindrance to interreligious dialogue.[12]

The pluralist position has all the shortcomings of the inclusivist theology of religions. Rahner's notion of the "anonymous Christian" arises from his Christian belief that Christians have no monopoly on the grace of the God revealed in Jesus Christ and from his desire to have Christian believers look upon non-Christians with charity and seriousness. And yet, despite Rahner's good intentions, the problems raised by Hick against inclusivism are quite real. Curiously, pluralist theories have the same problems. Pluralists, like inclusivists, enter into interreligious dialogue knowing more about other religious believers than these same believers know about themselves. Specifically, pluralists know that all religious believers, no matter what they might actually say about themselves, are really talking about the same transcendent Absolute. Also like inclusivists, pluralists know this *before* ever sitting down and talking with these religious believers.

In this respect, the pluralist position is unhelpful for Christians interested in responding to religious diversity. We are asked to believe that Buddhists and Muslims, Jews and Christians, at least those who do not subscribe to the pluralist point of view of Hick, Smith, and Samartha, all suffer from a limited understanding of themselves and their own religious tradition. This is not a particularly humble or open-minded way for a Christian to approach a Jew, a Muslim, or any other religious believer.

To his credit, John Hick has recognized the problem of pluralism's "higher knowledge" and has tried, unsuccessfully, to remedy the problem with his claim that pluralism is really a hypothesis. Wilfred Cantwell Smith is less aware of the difficulty and is not at all bashful in suggesting that his eyesight is God-like. "Evidently the new way that we are beginning to be able to see the global history of human kind," Smith assures us, "is presumably the way that God has seen it all along."[13] Stanley Samartha's appeal for a pluralistic theology of religions is couched not as a hypothesis but rather as a truth taken from a particular religious tradition, Hinduism. In this respect, of the three, Samartha's "pluralism" is actually a form of inclusivism. In Samartha's case, the inclusivism is Hindu, not Christian. Even "intolerant" religions like Christianity and Islam are ultimately included in the all-encompassing Mystery which has been revealed in the Hindu scriptures and expounded by Hindu sages.

The quasi-inclusivism of Hick, Smith, and Samartha means that pluralism presents a real difficulty for Christians seeking to be creative in responding to their religious neighbors who follow other religious paths. Hick's critics have a point: since the pluralists "know" that all religions are in fact expressions of one transcendental Absolute, everyone but the pluralists is blind. A view such as this does little to equip Christians for dealing creatively with their non-Christian neighbors, and, in fact, pluralism may do much to render the encounter between Christians and non-Christians sterile. This latter point can be seen by examining the second issue that confronts us when we realize that pluralism in fact is not a hypothesis.

Never Having to Change Your Mind

Christians who adopt the pluralist position may very well succeed in sealing themselves off from the transformative power of non-Christian religions. This is because pluralists have developed their view of religious diversity in such a way that they never have to change their minds about the meaning of religious diversity. Pluralists insulate their position on the ultimate unity of the many religions in such a way that no concrete fact can be offered that would indicate that the pluralist position in fact is not the case. The point here is *not* that Hick, Smith, and Samartha are arrogant or narrow-minded. They are not. Moreover, their good intentions are as laudable as those of the inclusivists. Despite the good intentions, however, pluralism does little to equip Christians with the skills necessary for transforming their own religious views in light of the teachings and wisdom of other religious traditions.

As we saw above in the discussion of whether or not Hick's thesis is a hypothesis or an assertion, no concrete fact can be raised that will require the pluralists to change their view of religious diversity. No matter how different one religion might prove to be from another religion, no matter how contradictory or incompatible, we know in advance that no religion really contradicts another religion ultimately. All religions are in fact expressions of the same transcendent Absolute. Christians who adopt this perspective on religious diversity never have to change their view of their non-Christian neighbors, no matter what those neighbors might have to say about themselves and their religious beliefs. For example, I once observed a conversation between a pluralist Christian and a Theravada Buddhist monk. The Buddhist, as one would expect, kept trying to explain that there was no equivalent to a creator God in his religious tradition. The pluralist Christian told me afterward that, despite what the monk was actually saying, she was sure that Buddhists and Christians were "really talking about the same thing." John Hick would be dismayed by this encounter. In my view, pluralism is the problem, not the solution.

This same problem is built into the pluralist proposals of Smith and Samartha. The problem is rooted in the sharp distinction the pluralists make between the one, transcendent Real, beyond all our concepts and images, and the many religions as interpretations of the Real. No matter how different one religion may be from another, all religions are responses to this same transcendent Absolute. Wilfred Cantwell Smith makes a similarly sharp distinction between our differing beliefs and our one common faith.[14] Beliefs are various, reflections of historical and cultural differences. Faith, on the other hand, is transcendent and comes to expression in beliefs without ever being able to be equated with belief. People with different beliefs share in the same faith. What would it take for Smith to change his mind on this issue? Is there any historical fact about a specific religion that would require Smith to conclude that not all religious believers share in the same, transcendent experience of faith after all?[15]

Stanley Samartha has unwittingly excused himself from the necessity of changing his mind as well. Like Hick and Smith, Samartha accomplishes this by means of his sharp distinction between what can be known and what cannot. In Samartha's case, we are told of the Mystery that is "the transcendent Center that remains always beyond and greater than apprehensions of it or even the sum total of those apprehensions."[16] This transcendent Absolute provides the basis for making a distinction between the unity of religions (*mataikya*) and the belief that ultimately religions do not contradict one another (*matavirodha*). When Christians and Muslims beg to differ, they are reprimanded for their arrogance and insensitivity and are required to expunge from their teachings all that does not comply with "traditional Indian pluralism." Here again we have an example of a pluralist whose views of religious diversity are curiously immunized against arguments to the contrary.

The issue here is not arrogance on the part of pluralists. The real problem has to do with the implications of the pluralist program for the second of our two criteria for a proper Christian response to religious diversity. Should Christians seeking to engage their non-Christian neighbors in a way that leads to a deepening of their religious understanding adopt a pluralist view of religious diversity? I think not. One sign of the spiritual maturity of a religious believer is the ability to change one's mind well—that is, to change religiously in a way that opens the believer up to a greater appreciation of truth and a greater understanding of his or her tradition and those of others. Perhaps the pluralists are correct. Perhaps all religions are in fact responses to a transcendent Absolute that lies beyond them all. On the other hand, exclusivists may be correct: one religious tradition is the true path and all the others are in error. Much more plausible is the view that religions are both similar and different in significant ways and that, therefore, religious believers have much to teach and to learn from one another. Adopting a pluralist position *prior* to entering into conversations with non-Christians, however, will not help Christians in learning from their non-Christian neighbors and may do much to prevent this creative response to religious diversity from ever getting off the ground.

Domesticating Differences

Another problem associated with the pluralist option for a theology of religions has to do with what I believe is an important issue for Christians today. We need to appreciate the real differences that distinguish one religion from another and reflect on what these differences might mean for our understanding of Christianity. In the pluralist perspective, the characteristics that distinguish one religion from another are *religiously* insignificant. No matter how dramatically different one religion may be from another, these differences have no bearing on that religion's ability to save its adherents. Despite their many differences, all religions lead to "salvation." Therefore, differences in doctrine become historical accidents or cultural preferences. In Smith's view, religious differences are matters of belief. They do not effect faith. For Samartha, they are but varying expressions of the same transcendent Mystery that lies beyond all historical particularities. All religions form a unity (*mataikya*) and, despite appearances, do not contradict one another (*matavirodha*).

Once again, pluralism shows itself to be unhelpful for Christians seeking creative responses to the fact of religious diversity today. Since religious differences are *religiously* insignificant, since all religions lead to salvation, these same religious differences are *theologically* insignificant as well. By "theologically insignificant" I mean that the strangeness of another religious tradition never really succeeds in requiring Christians to rethink the meaning of their own faith in Christ. This should be seen as a corollary to the fact that pluralism excuses us from changing our view of other religions. For a Christian who has adopted the pluralist program, religious differences do not require us to change our minds about the meaning of a non-Christian's religious tradition, and neither do religious differences require Christians to reinterpret their own tradition. The traits that distinguish one religion from another may be real, but they are of interest only to an anthropologist or historian. These differences are surprisingly insignificant for religious believers trying to take their religious neighbors seriously.

Let me offer some concrete examples. A religion like Theravada Buddhism counsels giving up belief in God as part of the path that leads to bliss. In contrast, Christians are called to believe in God with all their heart and mind and strength. Shinto surrounds the Japanese with thousands of local gods. In contrast, Christianity calls its followers to faith in the one God, in keeping with its Jewish roots. Confucianism teaches that T'ien (Heaven) does not enter actively into human affairs, but human affairs are to be directed in compliance with heaven's will. In contrast, Christianity teaches that God has entered into human affairs at a specific time and place. Pluralism does not ask Christians to think of these religious differences as opportunities to deepen their faith by revising their religious views. Instead, Christians are asked to believe that these different religious teachings are of no consequence to the human quest for salvation. Belief in the Christian God and Confucius's T'ien both lead to salvation—indeed, the *same* salvation.[17]

John Hick rejects this criticism of pluralism as a caricature of his own position.[18] Actual religious traditions hold very different views on matters of great importance. Muslims believe that Jesus of Nazareth was a Prophet, like Muhammad. Christians believe in Jesus as the incarnate Son of God. Hindus believe in the reincarnation of the soul after death. Christians teach the resurrection of the body. But even as Hick argues that pluralism recognizes the differences that distinguish the great religious traditions from one another, he takes a position that plays directly into the hand of his critics. First he notes that religions hold doctrines that are obviously in conflict and therefore different. Then he goes on to claim that "such differences are often indeed of great philosophical importance and elements within our respective theories about the universe, but they are not of great *religious*, i.e., soteriological importance." [emphasis in the original][19] Pluralists hold in common the need to deny religious differences any religious importance because that would suggest that religions might not be equally valid as paths leading to salvation. The differences distinguishing religions are allowed to remain, but only because they are gutted of any real significance.

This domestication of differences will result in a momentous loss for Christians. Pluralism has the unintended, but nevertheless real, effect of making non-Christian religious believers significantly less interesting to Christians. Once again pluralism's similarity with inclusivism is telling. Pluralists have a point when they criticize inclusivist theologies as strategies that effectively allow Christian believers to escape the necessity of taking other religious believers seriously. Pluralism, in keeping with its quasi-inclusivist character, is plagued with the same shortcoming. By rendering religious differences insignificant, pluralism effectively allows Christians to pass over the religious differences that distinguish them from their non-Christian neighbors without ever having to respond to them in any depth.

In its impact on the relationships between religious believers, this approach to religious diversity is not as tolerant as pluralists would have us believe. If the effect of the pluralist program is to render religious differences less significant, then non-Christian religions have little to teach Christian believers that is fundamentally important. Kenneth Surin, a particularly articulate critic of the pluralist position, notes that pluralists are sincere in their desire to give non-Christian religious views a place at the dialogue table. When non-Christians speak, however, "they are informed by our representative pluralists that what they say is in the final outcome not any different from what every and any other devout person professes."[20] "Tolerance" from the pluralist perspective means that the real differences that distinguish one religion from another are not really terrifying or challenging or intriguing. They are merely cultural or historical accidents or matters of ethnic preference. Above all, religious differences do not require us to return to our own religious tradition with new questions.

Many of the pluralists presume that a pluralist theology of religions is necessary for Christians to enter into dialogue with non-Christian believers authentically. Ironically, to the extent that pluralist theories of religious diversity serve to turn down the contrast on the differences distinguishing religions from one another, interreligious dialogue becomes a rather low-stakes affair. Genuine encounters between religious believers are kept safely in the shallows by the knowledge pluralism supplies in advance. The purpose of interreligious dialogue is hard to imagine from a pluralist perspective. Since religious differences are of no great religious or theological consequence, dialogue serves merely as an exercise in discerning how, in fact, we really are in agreement with one another, despite our differences. Since the end point of the encounter between religious traditions is safely under control, there is little danger that Christians will be taken by surprise or even be very puzzled by their conversations with their non-Christian neighbors. And, as noted above, they will never be required to change their mind about the real meaning of their neighbor's religion—or their own tradition, for that matter—at least in matters of fundamental importance.[21]

*   *   *

Pluralism, despite its claims for itself, is not helpful for Christians interested in responding to religious diversity in new and creative ways today. By rendering religious differences theologically uninteresting, pluralist theories do little to encourage Christians to learn more about non-Christian religious traditions on their own terms. Since radically contradictory religious beliefs are in reality differing interpretations of the same transcendent absolute, the encounter between religious believers is rendered less dangerous, but also less interesting than it would be otherwise. Pluralism fails the second of the two criteria for an adequate theology of religions. It does not assist Christians in responding creatively to the fact of religious diversity today. What about the first of the two criteria? Are the pluralist theories in keeping with the demands of the Christian tradition?

NOTES

1. Shubert Ogden, *Is There One True Religion or Are There Many?* (Dallas: Southern Methodist University Press, 1992), 78.

2. Gavin D'Costa served as editor of a collection of essays critical of the pluralist theories entitled *Christian Uniqueness Reconsidered: The Myth of a Pluralistic Theology of Religions* (Maryknoll, N.Y.: Orbis Books, 1990). This volume contains essays by Gavin D'Costa, M. M. Thomas, Francis X. Clooney, S.J., John Cobb, Jr., Wolfhart Pannenberg, Kenneth Surin, and others. For other criticisms of the pluralist model, see Ogden, *Is There One True Religion or Are There Many?* and J. A. Dinoia, *The Diversity of Religions: A Christian Perspective* (Washington, D.C.: The Catholic University of America Press, 1992); and S. Mark Heim, *Salvations: Truth and Difference in Religion* (Maryknoll, N.Y.: Orbis Books, 1995).

3. For Hick's use of this folktale, see John Hick, *God and the Universe of Faiths* (New York: St. Martin's Press, 1973), 140.

4. John Hick, *A Christian Theology of Religions: The Rainbow of Faiths* (Louisville, Ky.: Westminster John Knox Press, 1995), 49.

5. John Hick, *God Has Many Names: Britain's New Religious Pluralism* (London: Macmillan, 1980), 96.

6. John Hick, *An Interpretation of Religion: Human Responses to the Transcendent* (New Haven: Yale University Press, 1989), 235–36.

7. Ibid., 252–96.

8. Currently, the best critique of John Hick's pluralist "hypothesis" is Heim, *Salvations*.

9. Originally Hick put forth the principle of "eschatological verification" as an argument against religious skeptics who reject the idea that religious statements have any coherent meaning whatsoever because they can be neither verified nor falsified. See John Hick, *Faith and Knowledge* (New York: Macmillan, 1988), especially chapters 7 and 8. Only subsequently did he use this argument to support his claim that the pluralist position is in fact a hypothesis and not simply a raw assertion. For his most recent appeal to "eschatological verification," see *A Christian Theology of Religions*, 71–76.

10. John Hick, *Problems of Religious Pluralism* (New York: St. Martin's Press, 1985), 96–102.

11. S. Mark Heim, "The Pluralistic Hypothesis, Realism and Post-Eschatology," *Religious Studies* 28, no. 2 (1992): 207–19; see also *Salvations*, 35–40.

12. For Hick's critical assessment of Rahner, see *God and the Universe of Faiths*, 54–58.

13. Wilfred Cantwell Smith, *Toward a World Theology* (Philadelphia: Westminster Press), 18.

14. Wilfred Cantwell Smith, *Faith and Belief* (Princeton: Princeton University Press, 1979), 12.

15. Heim, *Salvations*, 57.

16. Stanley J. Samartha, "The Cross and the Rainbow: Christ in a Multi-religious Culture," in *The Myth of Christian Uniqueness: Toward a Pluralistic Theology of Religions,* ed. John Hick and Paul Knitter (Maryknoll, N.Y.: Orbis Books, 1987), 75.

17. For Hick's critics on this score, see P. Griffiths and D. Lewis, "On Grading Religions, Seeking Truth and Being Nice to People," *Religious Studies* 19 (1983): 75–80.

18. Hick, *Problems of Religious Pluralism*, 38–42.

19. Ibid., 88–95.

20. See Kenneth Surin in D'Costa, *Christian Uniqueness Reconsidered*, 200.

21. Ibid.

Chapter 6

LIBERATION OR PLURALISM?
PAUL KNITTER'S NEXT STEP

In the previous chapter, we looked at the difficulties that arise from adopting pluralist approaches to religious diversity such as those proposed by John Hick, Wilfred Cantwell Smith, and Stanley Samartha. We saw that the pluralist hypothesis is in fact an assertion about the relationship that all religions have with one another that needs to be judged on the basis of what we know about the similarities and the differences that link and separate religions. The pluralist position is alarming because of its propensity for domesticating the theologically very interesting differences that distinguish religious traditions. In the end, we found that the pluralist theories of Hick, Smith, and Samartha are not at all as pluralistic as they seem. Thus, they are not very helpful at all in equipping Christians to respond creatively to the opportunity our increased awareness of religious diversity offers to us today.

The many contributions of Paul Knitter to the debate over a pluralist theology of religions were not included in the previous chapter with good reason. Knitter's position on pluralism, or, more accurately, his developing position on pluralism, is considerably more complex than his three colleagues. Many of the difficulties that can be raised with the pluralist theories of Hick, Smith, and Samartha do not apply, or at least do not apply in the same way, to the writings of Paul Knitter. For this reason, Knitter requires a separate chapter. As with the other pluralists, the same two basic criteria for an adequate Christian response to the fact of religious diversity still apply. First, our response must be in keeping with the demanding richness of the Christian tradition. Second, the response needs to be creative so as to take advantage of the opportunity religious diversity poses for the enrichment of the religious lives of Christian believers today.

The Myth of God Incarnate: Adequate to the Tradition?

A common theme among pluralist theories is the call to abandon or at least reinterpret traditional Christian teaching about Jesus Christ. John Hick was among the first to call for a mythological view of the incarnation. For Hick, the divinity of Jesus is not to be taken literally as a historical fact. Rather, the incarnation is one particular way, the Christian way, of talking about the same salvation experienced by Muslims and Jews, Buddhists, Hindus, and others each in their own way. In keeping with the requirements of Wilfred Cantwell Smith's "world theology," Christians are not allowed to say anything about the incarnation that a Muslim or any other religious believer would not be able to accept as an expression of our common "faith." Given the fact that Muslims do not believe that Jesus was divine, Christianity's traditional belief in the incarnation of the Word will have to be revised considerably. Stanley Samartha states his position bluntly. When understood as the sole incarnation of the Word, Jesus Christ is merely the "tribal god" of the Christians and an offense to what he calls the "traditional pluralism" of India, making dialogue impossible. Christians should resist the temptation to make a god out of Jesus.[1]

As an exponent of pluralism, Paul Knitter has joined his voice to those of Hick, Smith, and Samartha in calling for a significant revision of Christianity's traditional understanding of Jesus Christ as the incarnation of the Word and unique savior of the world. Paul Knitter's proposal for a kingdom-centered understanding of Jesus Christ is the most highly developed and best argued of all the pluralists. Jesus preached the kingdom of God. The church, in contrast, preaches Jesus and has lost track of Jesus' original theocentric, religious vision. Now Christians must renew their own faith and prepare themselves for authentic dialogue by returning to the original concern of Jesus, God's liberating kingdom.[2]

Reading pluralist views of Jesus of Nazareth, one may be left with the impression that they are new. In fact, they hark back to the liberal Protestant views of Jesus of the nineteenth century. Like the older liberalism of theologians such as David Strauss and Adolf Harnack, pluralists presume that Christians must make their beliefs acceptable to the skeptical mood of the modern world. In the nineteenth century, Jesus had to be cleansed of his supernatural, miraculous, and divine qualities. By abandoning the divine Jesus affirmed by the patristic Church in the doctrine of the incarnation, the liberals hoped that the "real" Jesus of history would emerge to take his place. The "real" Jesus of history, a rabbinic wisdom figure, cleansed of any taint of the supernatural, would be more acceptable to the modern world than Jesus as the Christ, the Son of God and incarnate Word come down from heaven. In order to recover this Jesus of history, however, the old liberals had to take a scissors to the New Testament, leaving on the cutting room floor those passages from the New Testament they deemed unfit for a Christian believer eager to remain in step with the modern world. Paul's and John's proclamations of Jesus as the universal savior had to be strongly downplayed. Prominence was given instead to Jesus the preacher of the kingdom of God. The nineteenth-century liberals asked Christians to recognize that the New Testament is a calamitous distortion. In the Epistles of Paul and subsequently in the Gospels, the proclaimer unfortunately has become the proclaimed; the messenger has become the message. This was to be counted a momentous distortion of the original teachings of Jesus. In the New Testament and then in subsequent church history, most especially in the doctrine of the incarnation, the church's faith in Jesus as the Christ came to eclipse Jesus' original mission to announce the kingdom of God.

Today, the theological liberalism of the nineteenth century lives on in the pluralists and their calls for a theocentric theology of Jesus.[3] Reading the pluralists today gives one little sense of the bulk of New Testament scholarship since the heyday of the nineteenth-century liberals. This, at least, is Wolfhart Pannenberg's criticism of the theocentric Jesus.[4] Pannenberg's criticism is directed against Hick, and his arguments against a theocentric view of Jesus do not, in my view, apply to Paul Knitter's work to the same degree. Nevertheless, since the liberals, the bulk of New Testament scholarship has emphasized the "thread of continuity" linking Jesus' proclamation of the kingdom with the early church's proclamation of Jesus as Lord. Jesus is not only a witness to the coming kingdom of God, but the kingdom of God also becomes historically present in the life, death, and resurrection of the historical Jesus.[5] Therefore, the later church's interpretation of Jesus as the incarnation of the Word is not simply another example of the tendency of religious believers to divinize the founders of their respective religious communities, as Hick claims in his earlier work.[6] The doctrine of the incarnation is a consistent interpretation of Jesus' own understanding of himself and his mission.

What the theocentric understanding of Jesus wants to distinguish—namely, the reality of the kingdom and the one who proclaims it—Pannenberg wants to unite. The neat separation of the proclamation from the proclaimer demanded by the theocentric view of Jesus is not supported by contemporary New Testament scholarship. The kingdom of God (the message) comes into the world, at least in some anticipatory fashion, in the ministry of Jesus (the messenger). The notion of Jesus as the incarnation of God may be a later, more technical way of expressing this truth about the identity of Jesus, but it is fundamentally in continuity with the historical Jesus' understanding of himself.

> In fact, Jesus' emphasis on the anticipatory presence of God's kingdom in his own activity (Lk 11:20) involved his person in a way that essentially implies what later on was explicated by incarnational language and by titles like Son of God. But then, the uniqueness attributed to Jesus by the incarnational theology of the church was already characteristic of his own eschatological message and activity. Since the impending future of God was becoming present through him, there is no room for other approaches to salvation besides him. Those who relegate the claim to uniqueness to the "deification" of Jesus in later Christian interpretation do not take seriously the eschatological finality claimed by Jesus himself.[7]

Thus, Pannenberg disagrees with the pluralists when they say that the doctrine of the incarnation is merely a mythological way that Christians have for saying that Jesus is very important for them. Contrary to the pluralists, the doctrine of the incarnation is rooted in the historical Jesus himself, not in the wishful thinking of Christians who needed to deify the founder of their religion in the centuries that followed. Pannenberg believes this is the case because Christianity's "claim to uniqueness concerning the person of Jesus is bound up with his own eschatological message, especially with the eschatological finality of God's kingdom as becoming present in his activity."[8]

Much is at stake for Christians who wish to respond to the fact of religious diversity in ways that are adequate to the demands of their religious tradition and yet creative in recognizing the diversity of religions today as a real opportunity to deepen their faith. If we are to follow the pluralist program, Jesus, apparently, is really a human being and great teacher. He is divine only mythologically. This means that when Christians say that Jesus is human they are making a statement about a real historical fact. When they say that he is divine, they are speaking metaphorically. They are not referring to an actual historical event. Can Christians think of Jesus as a kind of Mohandas K. Gandhi, a truly great human being, and remain faithful to the demanding richness of the Christian tradition as our first criterion for responding to religious diversity demands? Is there not much that is lost in a mythological view of the incarnation?

The traditional Christian understanding of the incarnation is both richer and more demanding than the mythological view of the incarnation. In keeping with the original meaning of the doctrine of the incarnation, Christians have traditionally believed that Jesus Christ is fully divine and fully human. In other words, through the humanity of Jesus, the infinity of the living God, the God of Abraham, Isaac, and Jacob, has become present within history in a limited, tangible, indeed a *human* way. The doctrine of the incarnation does not mean that God has become present in the world *inside* a human being. In the humanity of Jesus, God has become present to us *as* a human being, a real person within history. The doctrine of the incarnation arose in the early history of the church in order to help Christians to resist two logical but far less demanding understandings of Jesus. First, the doctrine will not allow us to say that since Jesus is divine, he cannot be human. Second, the doctrine will not allow us to say that since Jesus is human, he cannot be divine. Both of these alternatives are easier to believe than the traditional doctrine itself. Perhaps in the ancient world the temptation was to believe that Jesus was really divine and therefore not really human. The mythological view of the incarnation, as promoted by the pluralists, reflects the modern tendency to believe that Jesus was really a human being and therefore could not be divine.

The doctrine of the incarnation, however, will not let us take either of these paths, even though they are easier to believe. The greatness of Christianity's traditional teaching about Jesus Christ can be seen in its dogged insistence that we undergo a kind of spiritual conversion in our understanding. In order to embrace deeply the truth that Jesus is fully divine and fully human, the presence of the infinite God within history in the life of a finite human being, we must change profoundly our understanding of what it means to be God and, therefore, what it means to be human. In effect I am saying that the traditional teaching about the divinity and humanity of Jesus is traditional because of the spiritual and ethical implications that flow from it. By believing in the traditional doctrine, namely, that the divine and the human are not irreconcilable opposites, the Christian believer is profoundly transformed. Spiritually and ethically, the traditional doctrine of the incarnation is both richer and more demanding than the mythological interpretation of it suggested by the pluralists. The theocentric Jesus is not adequate to the demanding richness of the Christian tradition.

The Myth of God Incarnate: Helpful for Christians Today?

Paul Knitter, however, makes a point that needs very much to be underscored. From its very beginnings, Christianity's understanding of Jesus has developed as a result of the Christian community's need to understand Jesus anew, generation after generation.[9] The great doctrinal achievements of the early church councils at Ephesis, Nicaea, and Chalcedon, in which Christians slowly hammered out the doctrine of the incarnation, are by no means an exception. In every era of the church's history, Christian believers have had to answer the question posed by Jesus to his disciples at Caesarea Philippi: Who do you say that I am? (Mk 8:27–30).

The present era of religious diversity is not an exception to this rule. In fact, historians may look back on this period of the church's history as especially creative in the development of our understanding of Jesus because of the conversations that are beginning to take place between Christians and believers from other faith traditions. At the core of Paul Knitter's efforts in regard to a theocentric understanding of Jesus is his commitment to liberation and to the renewal of Christianity through interreligious dialogue. If a theocentric understanding of Jesus does not respond adequately to the demands of the Christian tradition, is it helpful to Christians who seek to respond creatively to the fact of religious diversity today?

Paul Knitter has often warned that Christians cannot enter properly into dialogue with religious believers from other faiths until they have significantly revised their traditional beliefs about the uniqueness of Jesus of Nazareth.[10] The presumption that Christians should revise the theological understanding of their own tradition *before* entering into dialogue with other religious believers, however, does not seem very helpful to Christians concerned with responding in new ways to the fact of religious diversity. Perhaps a personal reflection will make this clear.

As a Christian theologian engaged in regular dialogues with Buddhists, I treasure my Buddhist friends not because they tell me what they think I want to hear but because they are faithful to the Dharma, the demanding teachings of the historical Buddha. Time and again, Buddhism has proved to be most stimulating to me as a Christian believer precisely where that religious tradition is most strange to me as a Christian. For my Buddhist friends to misrepresent their tradition in order to make it less strange and more acceptable to me would amount to a major loss. Buddhism can be enriching for Christians. The Dharma challenges us to rethink what we say about ourselves and about Jesus Christ. In some cases, Buddhist teachings have given me invaluable insights that have enabled me to understand my own faith in Jesus Christ in ways that I never would have imagined without my Buddhist friends. If my Buddhist dialogue partners were to sanitize their tradition in order to remove from it the teachings that might be troubling to me, I doubt seriously if my study of Buddhism would be as enriching to my Christian faith as in fact it is.

In their conversations with Muslims, should Christians want to hear watered-down versions of Islam designed to keep Christian feathers unruffled? Muslims believe that God's final and unsurpassable revelation to human beings is contained in the Qur'an, which was recited word for word in Arabic by the Prophet Muhammad, the last and greatest of God's prophets. Muslims speak of Muhammad as the "Seal of the Prophets" indicating that the Qur'an supersedes both the Torah and the Gospels as God's final and perfect revelation. Muhammad is not divine in any way. He is the one who recites what God has given him to say. Neither is Jesus divine. To say so is tantamount to polytheism for Muslims. Muslims honor Jesus as a prophet of God. The revelation given to Jesus, however, has been corrupted by merely human additions. Muslim belief starkly contradicts my belief in Jesus Christ as the historical incarnation of God. Should Christians expect a Muslim to check at the door all such beliefs as a condition for dialogue with Christians? The opposite would seem to be more sensible. Christians should be most interested in talking to Muslims about what it is that makes their religious tradition distinct from Christianity, including Muslim claims about the uniqueness of their religion. The points on which religious believers differ are precisely the issues of most value in interreligious dialogue.

What is true of Buddhism and Islam in interreligious dialogue is also true of Christianity: Why should a Muslim, a Buddhist, or anyone else want to talk with a Christian who has modified in advance her religious beliefs in keeping with what she *thinks* a conversation partner might find puzzling? Requiring religious traditions to revise their teachings *prior* to entering into dialogue may do much to render encounters between believers of differing religious traditions polite, though shallow, exercises in diplomacy. There should be an element of danger in dialogue. Our encounter with other believers should not leave us unscathed.

In the first centuries of the Christian movement, Christianity's encounter with Greek thought proved immensely important in the gradual development of church's recognition of Jesus as the incarnation of God within history. Today the church's encounter with non-Christian believers may prove to be equally stimulating for Christians as they seek to interpret anew the meaning of Jesus Christ in their lives. Christianity's encounter with non-Christian faiths is already puzzling. The encounter can also be transforming. To insist before entering into dialogue with non-Christian believers that Jesus is a myth or a model or a metaphor of a generic salvation and not a historical fact may very well prevent this transformation from happening.

And so it seems that the first criterion turns out to be connected intimately with the second criterion. In order to ensure that our response to religious diversity today will be truly creative and beneficial for the continued development of Christianity (second criterion), our understanding of Jesus Christ must be deeply faithful to the demanding richness of the tradition regarding the incarnation (first criterion). Our dialogue partners deserve no less.

This point can be illustrated with the following story. Some years ago, at a dialogue meeting between Christians and Buddhists, a Christian pluralist theologian presented his view of the centrality of Jesus Christ for Christians. Jesus was "merely a symbol" of a generic faith in the transcendent divine that Christians share with Buddhists. After the session, I spoke with a Buddhist friend. As I expected, she objected to the presumption that Buddhists believe in a transcendent divinity. But then she went on to ask me if Christians believe that Jesus is "merely a symbol." When I noted that most Christians believe that Jesus is the presence within history of the God of Abraham, my Buddhist friend sighed and asked why we were wasting time talking about what most Christians do not in fact believe.

Sōtéria or Justice?

A theocentric understanding of Jesus Christ by no means exhausts Paul Knitter's contribution to the debate on the theology of religions. What distinguishes Knitter's work from other pluralists is his emphasis on bringing the theology of liberation to bear on the problems posed for Christians by religious diversity. In my view, Knitter's deep personal commitment to the centrality of justice, for the suffering poor as well as the suffering earth, has gradually placed him in a position increasingly difficult for a pluralist to maintain. As a pluralist, Knitter wants to recognize the possibility (tantamount to the necessity) of there being more than one religious path that leads to salvation. But as a Christian whose religious commitments have been very much shaped by the theology of liberation, Knitter has had to recognize more than any of the other pluralists the need to assert a specific religious belief (in his case, God's demand for social justice) as a universal truth that calls the adequacy of other religious beliefs into question. Thus, his commitment to social justice as a paramount feature of what constitutes "salvation" requires that

Paul Knitter become a critic of religions that do not think in terms of promoting the well-being of the suffering poor and the suffering earth. Paul Knitter's commitment to liberation and his commitment to a pluralistic theology of religions are on a collision course.

Tensions such as we find within Paul Knitter can be creative, but how creative is this tension for Knitter? In his more recent writings, Knitter speaks of his personal odyssey from *ecclesiocentrism* (the belief that membership in the church is necessary for salvation) to *Christocentrism* (the necessity of belief in Christ), to *theocentrism* (belief in the Divine Ultimate beyond Jesus Christ) and now to *sōtériocentrism* (the idea of one salvation as a common feature uniting all the religious traditions).[11] Along with Paul Knitter, we might ask how helpful is the tension between his pluralism and his commitment to ecological and social justice for Christians looking for insights on how to respond creatively to the opportunities posed by religious diversity to their religious tradition today.

Implicit in Knitter's early work on a theocentric understanding of the historical Jesus and a mythological view of the doctrine of the incarnation was his confidence that an understanding of Jesus Christ that does not make absolute claims about him will allow Christians to bring together the need for a pluralistic theology of religions and the theology of liberation's insistence on the priority of social justice. The theocentric Jesus is witness not to himself but to God's liberating activity in bringing about the kingdom. At the same time, the theocentric Jesus is but one way of modeling the universally human experience of salvation *(sōtéria)*. The traditional understanding of the incarnation as God's unique and unequaled entry into human history has been used not only as an ideology to support the violence of the Christian missionary movement but also as a justification of Western colonialism, the cross accompanied by the sword.

In Knitter's later work the urgencies of the theology of liberation are increasingly evident. Knitter hopes that the theology of liberation can benefit from pluralism's appreciation of the liberating elements in all religious traditions. Even more so, Knitter hopes that the pluralistic theology of religions can benefit by recognizing the "preferential option for the poor" and ecological concern for the earth as the key issues for interreligious dialogue.[12] The purpose of a pluralistic theology of religions and interreligious dialogue is to bring religious believers together to address the reality of the suffering poor and the suffering ecology and to work for social justice.[13]

As Paul Knitter's concern for the theology of liberation has become more prominent, so also has the tension between his commitment to justice as a particular interpretation of what salvation is and his pluralist view that all religions make salvation available to their followers. Nowhere is the tension more clearly seen than in Knitter's notion of *sōtéria,* which, of necessity, he must define broadly as "eco-human well being" or "human and ecological well being."[14] Religions may be vastly different in other respects, but all religions can agree on the well-being of the human community and the ecological health of the earth.[15]

Sōtéria remains broadly described. The precise meaning of *sōtéria* is never made sufficiently clear. This too is an indication of the tension between Knitter's pluralism and his commitment to social justice. On the one hand, *sōtéria* is to be taken as a practical suggestion for a topic for discussion at interreligious dialogues. Therefore, *sōtéria* acts merely as "a beacon that points us in a particular direction and then provides us with enough light to discover what there is to find as we move forward."[16] The precise meaning of the term can be spelled out only through the actual practice of interreligious dialogue.

On the other hand, Knitter claims that *sōtéria* is not to be taken as merely the material well-being of the earth and its peoples. *Sōtéria* is the "well being of humans and the planet that results from feeling and living the immanent-transcendent Mystery."[17] All religions are in agreement that in order to promote the well-being of the earth and its peoples, "we will have to acknowledge or wake up to the *divinum* that animates or transcends the human and the cosmic."[18] Because of this Mystery, which transcends all the religions and becomes available through them, all religions can affirm a sense of "global responsibility" for the earth and its many peoples. *Sōtéria* apparently reflects the nature of religion in general.[19] This notion, therefore, is clearly a cousin to John Hick's "Ultimate Reality," Stanley Samartha's "Mystery," and Wilfred Cantwell Smith's universally human experience of "faith." Every religion in the world can recognize itself in *sōtéria* because every religion shares in a concern for the well-being of all and the ecological fate of the earth. Or, at the very least, they ought to be so concerned.

Should the concern for social justice be taken as a transcendent metaphysical Absolute common to all religions or a practical suggestion as a topic for interreligious dialogue? As was the case with Knitter's mythological view of the incarnation, much is at stake here. No one should have any quarrel with the idea of social justice or "eco-human well being" as an important and worthwhile topic for believers from different traditions to explore in interreligious dialogues. However, if *sōtéria* is a metaphysical absolute that lies behind all the religions, even those religions that do not recognize this fact, Knitter not only has the same problems we have seen with Hick, Smith, and Samartha and their candidates for a metaphysical absolute behind the religions; Knitter has another problem as well. Knitter would have us believe that religions are more alike as forces for social liberation than they are as doctrinal systems. In other words, Knitter would have us believe that religions say very different things about God (or the nonexistence of God) and how to worship God, as well as about sin, forgiveness, grace, life after death, and countless other topics. But despite all these differences, they all make one salvation (interpreted differently) available to their adherents and this salvation should be understood in very worldly terms: "human and ecological well being."

Is *sōtéria* only a topic for interreligious dialogue or the transcendental unity beyond all the religions? Major problems in Knitter's program for a theology of religions that is both pluralist and liberationist begin to show themselves once we move from the realm of generalities to concrete examples, a move that Knitter almost never makes.

Let us look at a concrete example. "Concern for *sōtéria*," Knitter claims, "naturally and automatically creates *solidarity*...."[20] This seems very unlikely. Daniel Berrigan, a Jesuit priest and political activist, has said repeatedly that Christians must work against the social structures of any society that is not yet the kingdom of God. His Christian commitment to the social demands of the gospel has led Father Berrigan to various acts of civil disobedience in resisting U.S. militarism. Despite his many efforts to challenge social structures and transform his society, Father Berrigan is well aware that the kingdom he works for is not of his own creation. God's kingdom will come with the second coming of Christ.

The Ayatollah Khomeini was also a critic of his society, Iran under the regime of the Shah. Like Daniel Berrigan's vision of the kingdom of God as a social ideal, the Ayatollah Khomeini's Shi'ite Muslim beliefs called him to be an activist working against any society that was not yet an Islamic society. Similar to Daniel Berrigan's understanding of the kingdom of God as an act of God arriving only at the second coming of Christ was the Ayatollah's belief, in accordance with his own Shi'ite Muslim teaching, that a truly Islamic society will arise only with the coming of the "Hidden Imam," at the end of time.

Are we to take the obvious parallels in these two decidedly different views of what constitutes the well-being of humans and the planet as varying expressions of *sōtéria*? Both the Ayatollah and Father Berrigan are religious believers acting out of their respective religious visions of a ideal society, even though many Christians and many Muslims may wish to quarrel with their interpretations of the Gospels and the Qur'an. Yet it seems very unlikely that these religious activists, both of whom would agree that they are acting for the well-being of humans and the planet, would want to embrace one another as comrades-in-arms. Yet Paul Knitter tells us that "concern for *sōtéria* naturally and automatically creates *solidarity*...."[21]

In fact, religions seem to differ significantly in their social vision of what constitutes human well-being in no small part because their religious doctrines are so different. Christianity's concern with social justice, for example, is rooted in its hope for the coming of the kingdom of God at the end of time when "the meek shall inherit the earth." Confucianism, on the other hand, tends to speak more of harmony than of justice. Confucius's vision of a harmonious society is based on the "five relations" in which inferiors are required to be compliant and superiors are required to be responsible. Hinduism thinks of human well-being in terms of the proper and harmonious relations among the castes.

Knitter's strong commitments to the ideals of the theology of liberation might suggest that he would conclude that Father Berrigan, and not the Ayatollah, is actually in touch with *sōtéria*. But to do so carries with it a very unpluralistic result: Knitter would have to maintain that some religious people are simply wrong in their religious beliefs, especially their beliefs about what counts most in matters religious—for Knitter, *sōtéria*. As a matter of fact, this is exactly what Paul Knitter maintains. Religions that do not address, as their primary concern, the poverty and the political repression of the world cannot be considered "authentic." Dialogue with such religions risks decaying into a "purely mystical pursuit" in which "something essential is missing."[22]

The point to be taken here is that Knitter's commitment to social justice and the theology of liberation requires him to be especially wary of the easygoing relativism that can so easily become the fruit of pluralist theories of religious diversity that speculate about a transcendent Absolute behind all the religions.[23] Knitter is well aware that the ruling classes find this kind of relativism congenial because it means that no religious believer can ever demand of them that they change their behavior. Since all religions are really saying the same thing in different ways, bourgeois Christianity must be okay as well. No one is really wrong religiously, including the oppressors. Knitter resists this relativism by holding up a very particular religious value as paramount: social justice. But the more he does so, the more his theology of liberation is in conflict with the pluralist theories of Hick, Smith, and Samartha. This is a tension that will not be resolved until Paul Knitter makes a break with the view that all religions are expressions of a transcendent Absolute.

Where to Draw the Line

Paul Knitter insists on the urgency of the need to address poverty and ecological disaster. For this reason, he does not believe that mutual understanding among religions is sufficient as a goal for interreligious dialogue. Today we must make judgments about religions, rejecting some and accepting others. The ideals of the Christian theology of liberation provides Knitter with a place to stand for making judgments, severe judgments in some cases, regarding the acceptability and even the authenticity of religions.[24] Curiously, Knitter thinks he can make these judgments without surrendering his pluralist position. He does this by appealing to his notion of *sōtéria*, and here again the ambiguity in the notion of *sōtéria* is apparent.

By evaluating religions based on their commitment to *sōtéria*, in Knitter's view, the real similarities and the real differences linking and separating religions will become more apparent. In a liberation theology of religions, the boundary lines dividing religious believers will run not *between* religious traditions but *across* them. Typically, Christianity is seen as a separate religion from Islam or Hinduism. Knitter believes that the lines now need to be drawn between religious believers who support social justice and those who do not. This means that Christians, Muslims, Hindus, and others who are committed to social justice will find solidarity with one another and oppose religious believers from their own tradition who do not share in their ideal of social justice.

In this regard, Knitter quotes Harvey Cox with approval. When believers enter into interreligious dialogue with a sense of the urgency of social justice, we will begin to look at the relationship between religious traditions in new ways.

> Similarities and differences [between religions] which once seemed important fade away as the real differences—between those whose sacred stories are used to perpetuate domination and those whose religion strengthens them for the fight against domination—emerge more clearly.[25]

Here, however, a note of caution needs to be sounded. The boundary lines separating religious believers may not be redrawn as radically as Paul Knitter suggests. Like the other pluralists, Knitter makes sizable demands on all religious believers. John Hick asks that all religious believers consign to the realm of mythology anything about their religion that would distinguish it from other religions as absolute and normative for all. Wilfred Cantwell Smith, in order to have a world theology, asks that religious believers say nothing about their own tradition that a believer from another tradition would find disagreeable. Paul Knitter asks that all religious believers judge their spiritual practices and the teachings of their tradition not in terms of their fidelity to their scriptures or to the original teaching of the founders but rather in terms of their social effects.

In doing so, Knitter's program tends to favor some religions over others. If we were to act on Knitter's proposal for a liberation theology of religions, some believers would be affected in dramatic ways, while others would not be very affected at all. On the whole, religions with more clearly defined "prophetic" dimensions, such as Judaism, Christianity, and Islam, are favored, while religions that traditionally have been more "mystical" or "devotional" in character—Hinduism is an obvious example—

are found wanting. Knitter does not see this uneven effect as a form of the intolerance, which any self-respecting pluralist should find abhorrent.[26] For example, traditional Brahmanical Hinduism, which supports the caste system in India, is presumably not an authentic religion in Knitter's view. Paul Knitter's own brand of politically committed Christianity, on the other hand, moves to the head of the class. The Brahman, before he is permitted at the dialogue table, will require a more soul-searching "conversion" to the liberationist point of view than, say, Harvey Cox, a Christian who is in agreement with Paul Knitter on the paramount importance of social criticism as the sign of religious authenticity.

Knitter's Future: Pluralist or Liberationist?

Is Paul Knitter's liberationist theology of religions in fact all that pluralistic? Knitter continues to identify himself with the pluralists but admits that he is increasingly uncomfortable with the term.[27] This discomfort is a virtue. His deeply held Christian commitments to social activism have placed him on what is turning out to be a collision course with those who want to maintain that all religions are variant expressions of the same transcendent reality. Knitter has criticized the Christian doctrine of the incarnation for being an ideology serving to justify Western imperialism in the Third World. In turn, Knitter has been criticized for making "justice" into a new religious absolute that is as entangled in Western imperialism as any other Christian doctrine. Knitter denies the charge.[28] But his strong commitment to the paramount importance of social justice inevitably entangles him in very unpluralistic arguments.

Knitter's recent publications provide a particularly obvious example. Knitter's commitment to the pluralist model requires him to believe that *sōtéria* is available to believers through all the great religions of the world. But his commitment to the theology of liberation requires him to make unpluralistic judgments against religious believers who support the oppression of the poor. This irony is dramatically visible in the comments he offers about the *Bhagavad Gita*, arguably the most beloved of Hindu scriptures. Over the centuries, the *Gita* has been manipulated by the Brahman upper castes in India to obscure its original, anticaste message.[29] The *Gita* is really a document that is liberationist, countercultural, and politically destabilizing. Here is an American, inspired by his deeply held Christian belief in social justice, criticizing Hindus for their improper reading of their own scriptures. Knitter's reading of the *Gita* may be right. But right or wrong, Knitter's position bears little resemblance to the pluralism of Hick, Smith, and Samartha any longer.

The conflict Knitter's liberationist theology of religion generates with Stanley Samartha's pluralist program is especially ironic. As a pluralist concerned about the "imperialism" of the Christian missionary movement in India, Samartha presumably would be very much opposed to Knitter's liberationist commitments, although this in fact may not be his view. According to Samartha's account of traditional Indian pluralism, all religions are expressions of the same transcendental Mystery beyond them all. Samartha demands that Christians abandon their normative claims over other religions lest Christianity upset the delicate social harmony of religions in India. Ironically, India's "social harmony" is what Knitter believes "authentic religions" must destabilize. What constitutes "human and ecological well being" for an American inspired by the ideals of the Christian theology of liberation may seem strangely like neocolonialism in Riyadh and Beijing or even a village in rural India.

* * *

I do not mean to imply that Paul Knitter is wrong in his attempt to bring the concerns of the theology of liberation to bear in the development of the theology of religions. I do claim, however, that the more insistent he becomes about liberation, the less pluralistic he is forced to become. This is a virtue, not a vice. By entering into dialogue with Hindus in India, Knitter may come face to face with people who do not share his liberationist ideals. They have other ideals that are rooted in their own, deeply held religious beliefs. In this regard, Knitter and traditional Brahmans have much to talk about. But if we presume that all religions are in touch with a transcendent Absolute like *sōtéria*, and when those believers who do not subscribe to Knitter's particularly Christian notions of social justice are dismissed as "inauthentic," then Knitter's pluralism has absolved him of taking religious differences seriously. The traditional Brahman may rightly be excluded from the conversation.

NOTES

1. For Hick's views on the incarnation, see John Hick, in *The Myth of God Incarnate*, ed. John Hick and Paul Knitter (Philadelphia: Westminster Press, 1977), passim; also idem, *God Has Many Names: Britain's New Religious Pluralism* (Philadelphia: Westminster Press, 1982), 69–75, idem, *An Interpretation of Religion: Human Responses to the Transcendent* (New Haven: Yale University Press, 1989), 343–61; idem, *The Metaphor of God Incarnate* (London: SCM Press, 1993). For Smith, see Wilfred Cantwell Smith, *Toward a World Theology* (Philadelphia: Westminster, 1981), 170–79. For Samartha, see Stanley J. Samartha, "The Cross and the Rainbow: Christ in a Multi-religious Culture," in *The Myth of Christian Uniqueness: Toward a Pluralistic Theology of Religions*, ed. John Hick and Paul Knitter (Maryknoll, N.Y.: Orbis Books, 1987), 79.

2. Paul Knitter, *No Other Name?* (Maryknoll, N.Y.: Orbis Books, 1985), 169–204.

3. For a criticism of Wilfred Cantwell Smith as a latter-day liberal Protestant, see Langdon Gilkey, "A Theological Voyage with Wilfred Cantwell Smith," *Religious Studies Review* 7, no. 4 (October 1981): 298–306, especially 304–6.

4. Wolfhart Pannenberg, "Religious Pluralism and Conflicting Truth Claims: The Problem of a Theology of the World Religions," in *Christian Uniqueness Reconsidered: The Myth of a Pluralistic Theology of Religions*, ed. Gavin D'Costa (Maryknoll, N.Y.: Orbis Books, 1990).

5. The work of the "Jesus Seminar," of course, is an exception to this rule. Part of the notoriety of the seminar is due to the fact that its findings concerning Jesus are presented as radical when in fact they have a great deal in common with the thought of nineteenth-century liberals. For works of the Jesus Seminar, see, inter alia, the following: John Dominic Crossan, *The Essential Jesus: Original Sayings and Earliest Images* (San Francisco: Harper, 1994); idem, *The Historical Jesus: The Life of a Mediterranean Jewish Peasant* (San Francisco: Harper, 1991); and idem, *Jesus: A Revolutionary Biography* (San Francisco: Harper, 1994); Robert Funk, ed., *The Acts of Jesus: The Search for the Authentic Deeds of Jesus* (San Francisco: Harper, 1998); idem, *The Five Gospels: The Search for the Authentic Words of Jesus* (New York: Macmillan, 1993); Burton Mack, *The Lost Gospel: The Book of Q and Christian Origins* (San Francisco: Harper, 1993). For a criticism of the Jesus Seminar as merely an echo of the nineteenth-century quest for the historical Jesus, see Richard Hays, "The Corrected Jesus," in *First Things* 43 (May 1994): 43–48.

6. John Hick, "Jesus and the World Religions," in *The Myth of God Incarnate*, 169–70.

7. Pannenberg, "Religious Pluralism and Conflicting Truth Claims," 100–101.

8. Ibid., 101.

9. Knitter, *No Other Name?* 177–82.

10. Ibid., 165–68. John Hick also takes this position; see Hick, *God Has Many Names*, 80–97.

11. For accounts of his intellectual journey from exclusivism to inclusivism to pluralism, see Paul Knitter, *Jesus and the Other Names: Christian Mission and Global Responsibility* (Maryknoll, N.Y.: Orbis Books, 1996), 1–14, idem, *One Earth Many Religions: Multifaith Dialogue and Global Responsibility* (Maryknoll, N.Y.: Orbis Books, 1995), 36

12. Paul Knitter, "Toward a Liberationist Theology of Religions," in *The Myth of Christian Uniqueness*, ed. John Hick and Paul Knitter (Maryknoll, N.Y.: Orbis Books, 1987), passim.

13. Knitter, *One Earth Many Religions*, 58.

14. Ibid., 98, 185 n. 17.

15. Ibid., 17.

16. Ibid., 98.

17. Ibid., 99.

18. Ibid. In a footnote Knitter acknowledges that those who follow nontheistic religions such as Buddhism will not be comfortable with a term like *divinum*.

19. Ibid., 97.

20. Ibid., 79.

21. Ibid.

22. Knitter, "Toward a Liberationist Theology of Religions," 180.

23. Knitter is forthright in acknowledging the problem of relativism implicit within the various proposals for a pluralist theory of religion. See Knitter, *One Earth Many Religions*, 30, and "Toward a Liberationist Theology of Religions," 181.

24. John Hick has also spent a great deal of effort in the attempt to resist relativism in his pluralistic theory of religious diversity by offering criteria for "grading religions," although Hick's criteria are not as explicitly political as Paul Knitter's liberation-theology approach. See John Hick, "On Grading Religions," *Religious Studies* 17 (1981): 451–67.

25. Knitter, "Toward a Liberationist Theology of Religions," 188. For the original text, see Harvey Cox, *Religion in the Secular City: Toward a Postmodern Theology* (New York: Simon & Schuster, 1984), 238.

26. Knitter, *One Earth Many Religions*, 23, 30.

27. Ibid., 16.

28. For the criticism of justice as an ideological religious absolute, see S. Mark Heim, *Salvations: Truth and Difference in Religion* (Maryknoll, N.Y.: Orbis Books, 1995), 92. For Knitter's denial of the charge, see *One Earth Many Religions*, 97.

29. Knitter, *One Earth Many Religions*, 110.

Chapter 7

EXPERIMENTING WITH COMPARISON

The debate over the question of a theology of religions adequate for the world of vast religious diversity that Christians face today has been lively to say the least. Now, however, we need to recognize that the debate has come to an impasse. What might be called the prelude to the debate, the discussion between exclusivists like Karl Barth and inclusivists like Karl Rahner has shifted in recent years to the controversy over pluralist theologies of religion. This book is written out of the conviction that today Christians need to develop skills for living responsibly and creatively with their non-Christian neighbors. In regard to this requirement, all three of the basic options for a theology of religions have been found wanting.

Now there is a new development having to do with Christianity and its relationship to other religions, a development that holds great promise for Christians who wish to think about their religion in relationship to their non-Christian neighbors. A small number of Christian theologians are beginning to argue that the time has come to turn away from the controversy over a pluralist theology of religions. These Christian theologians are turning away from the question of a theology of religions, pluralist or otherwise, and are beginning to think about Christianity in relation to other religions comparatively.

Comparative theology is the attempt to understand the meaning of Christian faith by exploring it in the light of the teachings of other religious traditions. The purpose of comparative theology is to assist Christians in coming to a deeper understanding of their own religious tradition. Doing Christian theology comparatively means that Christians look upon the truths of non-Christian traditions as resources for understanding their own faith. In this respect, I believe that comparative theology is a better way for Christians to respond creatively to the fact of religious diversity today.

Before discussing comparative theology as an alternative to the theology of religions, which I will do in the following chapter, I want to offer two examples of doing Christian theology comparatively. The first example brings together a Hindu story about divine love and a story of Jesus, familiar to all Christians, the parable of the Prodigal Son. The second example brings together a Zen Buddhist text about the relationship of life and death with New Testament passages about the resurrection.

Krishna and the Milkmaids

Among the most popular gods in India is Krishna. His pranks as a child are familiar throughout the subcontinent. The heroic deeds of his later life have been recited in poem and celebrated in festival by rich and poor alike for almost two thousand years. Krishna is also remembered as an ideal lover, the sweetness and the passion of divine love.[1]

One of the most popular of all the stories about Krishna has to do with his exploits as a lover of the *gopi*s or milkmaids. In one often-retold episode, Krishna appears late one night outside the village of the *gopi*s in the forest. Making enchanting music with his flute, Krishna lures the *gopi*s out of their houses in order to dance a circle-dance with his lovers. On hearing the music, the *gopi*s awaken and hurry into the forest to be with their lover.

> The women, whose souls were conquered by Krishna, did not have any more attachments to the world. In spite of the impediments caused by their husbands, relatives, parents and others, they hurried toward Krishna.[2]

As lovers, however, the *gopis* are jealous. They want to be with their lover and to possess his love secretly and for themselves alone. As the *gopis* arrive and begin to think that they are in competition for the attentions of Krishna, they are filled with pride and covetousness. In their foolishness, each *gopi* tries to hoard Krishna for herself. With this, Krishna disappears from their midst. Happily, this punishment does not last long. As the *gopis* begin to lament the loss of their lover and repent of their foolishness, Krishna reappears with his flute and the dance resumes. Now, however, Krishna's love for the *gopis* is not only tender but skillful. Krishna miraculously multiplies himself so that for every *gopi* around the circle, there is Krishna, the passionate lover gazing into the eyes of his beloved. Krishna's love is such that there is plenty to go around, no matter how many *gopis* may have come into the forest to join in the dance. In the background, behind the cavorting lovers, flows the Yamuna, the river of life.

Krishna's disappearing act teaches the *gopis* a worthwhile lesson. Those who try to possess divine love for themselves succeed only in making it disappear from their life. Krishna's love is passionate for each and every one of us, but we must not become prideful and possessive over our lover. Divine love will be ours to savor only to the extent that we do not try to monopolize it. Jealousy, competitiveness, and possessiveness make the divine disappear. Krishna cannot be possessed. We can only dance with him. Divine love cannot be hoarded, but it is infinitely skillful in offering itself to us.[3]

The Parable of the Prodigal Son

How might this Hindu story become a resource for Christians seeking to understand their own faith more deeply? Certainly, the urge to "possess" God and hoard God's love for ourselves is not a problem restricted to Hindu believers. Christians know this temptation too. The sin of hoarding God is readily apparent in the anti-Judaism that asserts "God does not hear the prayer of a Jew!" In Northern Ireland some Christians say the same thing about Catholics; others say this of Protestants. Some Christians are boisterous in asserting how sure they are that they have been saved by the love of Jesus. With the same fearful certainty, however, they assert that others are not saved. What if Christians tried to imagine the love of Jesus the way Hindus imagine of love of Krishna? Should Christians think of Jesus the way Hindus think of Krishna, that is to say, as the divine flute player who wants only to meet his lovers late at night and dance with them until dawn?

The story of Krishna and the *gopi*s helps Christians to read their own scriptures in new ways. In one of his most famous stories, Jesus tells us that "A man had two sons…" (Lk 15:11). The younger of the two demanded his share of the estate of his father and went off to a distant land "where he squandered his inheritance on a life of dissipation." Eventually, the son became destitute. "Coming to his senses" at last, the son decided to return to his father with the idea of working on the land as a hired hand. As he returned, the father caught sight of him and "was filled with compassion." Running out to meet his son, the father "embraced him and kissed him." Then the father said to his servants,

> Quickly! bring the finest robe and put it on him; put a ring on his finger and sandals on his feet. Take the fattened calf and slaughter it. Then let us celebrate with a feast because this son of mine was dead and has come to life again; he was lost and has been found. (Lk 15:22–24)

Too often, Christians end the story here, with the father's warm reception of his son and the preparations for the banquet. However, this is not the way Jesus ends his story. As the banquet began, the elder son came in from working on the land and heard the sound of music and dancing. A servant told him that his younger brother had returned and that his father had killed the fattened calf in order to celebrate. The son "became angry, and refused to enter the house." So "his father came out and pleaded with him." After hearing his elder son's complaint, the father spoke these words to him: "My son, you are here with me always; everything I have is yours. But we must celebrate and rejoice, because your brother was dead, and has come to life again; he was lost, and has been found" (Lk 15:31–32).

The temptation to leave off the last part of Jesus' story is worth reflecting on. Moreover, the Hindu story of Krishna and the *gopi*s can act as a kind of guide in this matter. The part about the older, responsible brother growing angry with his father is by no means an extra comment that is not really part of the main story. When we read Jesus' parable in light of the story of Krishna and the *gopi*s, the main point of the parable of the Prodigal Son seems to shift from a focus on the irresponsible younger brother to the older brother standing outside the banquet. True, most of the parable is given over to a description of the irresponsible behavior of the younger son and the rejoicing of the father at his son's return. At the end of the story, however, the older, responsible son is standing outside the banquet with a decision to make: Shall he join in the celebration or not? The father clearly loves both of his sons. The older brother does not want to accept this. Justice is at stake here. "Look, all these years I served you," he says to his father, "and not once did I disobey your orders; yet you never gave me even a young goat to feast on with my friends. But when your son returns who swallowed up your property with prostitutes, for him you slaughter the fattened calf"(Lk 15:29–30). In justice, the father should not welcome home the younger son as he has. In Jesus' story, however, the father is not interested in justice. He is interested only in the fact that his younger son was "dead and has come to life again" and that he was "lost and has been found" (Lk 15:32).

Normally, in commenting on Jesus' story, Christian biblical scholars emphasize the father's joy over the repentance of the younger son. This certainly makes sense. The fifteenth chapter of the Gospel of Luke begins with the murmuring of the scribes and the Pharisees over Jesus' association with tax collectors and sinners (Lk 15:1–2) and continues with two parables about rejoicing over what had been lost (Lk 15:3–10). Then comes the story of the Prodigal Son. The rejoicing of the father over his lost son fits right in with the theme of the other two parables that make up chapter.[15] Reading the parable of the Prodigal Son with the Hindu story of Krishna and the *gopi*s in mind does not change this. The Hindu story, however, helps Christians to see aspects of Jesus' parable which otherwise go unnoticed.

For example, the older son in the story is concerned about justice. The father in Jesus' story, however, is concerned with love, not justice. He loves not only his son who is dutiful and responsible but also his son who is an irresponsible fool. Like the father in Jesus' parable, God loves irresponsible fools. When it comes to other people and their moral failures, very often we are like this older son, wanting God to be more focused on justice than on love. But like Krishna, dividing himself repeatedly in order to be with each and every one of his beloved *gopis*, Jesus' parable suggests that God pours out his love on the dutiful and the irresponsible alike. God loves welfare frauds and corrupt politicians, fanatics and atheists. The truth is that God loves people *we* do not love. Furthermore, the more we insist that God does not love those who are less moral or less faithful or less dutiful than ourselves, the more divine love disappears from our own lives, like Krishna disappearing from the midst of his selfish *gopis*.

Biblical scholars have suggested that the title Christians have given to Jesus' story, "The Prodigal Son," should be changed. The story of Krishna and the *gopis* lends support to this idea. *Prodigal* means "extravagantly wasteful" or "profligate" and, to be sure, the younger brother is a prodigal son. But the *father* in Jesus' story is prodigal as well. The father is extravagantly wasteful in the way he loves his irresponsible son. The older brother recognizes this and is troubled by it. The story might be renamed "The Prodigal Father," because Jesus wants us to understand that God's extravagantly wasteful love, poured out as it is on sinners, confronts us all with a decision: either we can become extravagant lovers like God or we can stay out in the cold while the banquet unfolds inside our Father's house.

Perhaps one sign that we are fallen is that we have a deep-seated fear that there may not be enough of God's love to go around. Dorothy Day, the founder of the Catholic Worker Movement and its "houses of hospitality," knew that God wants to dance with all his lovers, including the "guests" who came for a meal in her soup kitchens. In the Gospels, Jesus is criticized by his contemporaries because he associates with tax collectors and sinners. Anyone who has friends such as these cannot be a man of God. Jesus' God, however, dances with tax collectors. He plays his flute for sinners. Moreover, as in the Krishna story, divine love disappears from our lives when we attempt to exclude others from that love. In telling us this parable, Jesus confronts us with the fact that our human sense of justice cannot begin to fathom the prodigal love of God. Reading Jesus' parable with the Hindu story as a guide suggests that we should identify with the older brother, standing outside the banquet hall with a decision to make. Will we come to the banquet or stay out in the cold, dark night of our anger and sense of justice?

Krishna, Christ, and the Pluralists

Are Christians and Hindus talking about the same God? Are Christ and Krishna both images of a transcendent Absolute that lies beyond both Christianity and Hinduism? Questions such as these arise from the standpoint of the theology of religions. Doing theology comparatively, on the other hand, puts this kind of question aside and asks how Hinduism can teach Christians to understand their religion in new ways. For this reason, the differences between Christianity and Hinduism are as instructive as the similarities.

Hindus think of Krishna as an *avatar* of the great divinity Vishnu. The word *avatar* means "divine descent." Vishnu, who is utterly beyond all our attempts to imagine or conceptualize, has made himself visible and accessible here in the world in no fewer than ten different *avatars*. He is the divine child as well as Rama, the heroic adventurer in the *Ramayana*. He is the dwarf who saves the world and of course, the flute-playing lover of *gopis*. Some Hindus also think of Jesus and the Buddha as *avatars* of Vishnu. Christians have no monopoly on inclusivist theologies. All of these *avatars* are part of the world of illusion. They are not real. They are mere appearances of Lord Vishnu, who is beyond the illusory world.

Is Jesus, like Krishna, an *avatar* of Vishnu? Is Vishnu a word Hindus use to name the same transcendent Reality that Christians call God? This does not seem to be the case. Christians say that Jesus is the incarnation of the living God. Hindus say that Krishna is an *avatar* of Vishnu. Jesus of Nazareth was a real, historical human being, a first-century Palestinian Jew. In calling Jesus the incarnation of the living God, Christians believe that Jesus is the God of Abraham, Isaac, and Jacob become a real, historical human being, not God taking on the appearance of a human being. At the same time, the incarnation means that a real human being has become divine within history. In fact, Christianity has a long history of struggling against those who insist on claiming that Jesus was truly divine but not truly or at least not fully human. To think of Jesus as an *avatar* of Abraham's God appearing here on earth would not be in accordance with the time-honored history of Christian belief. Hinduism and Christianity are different in this regard. They do not seem to be talking about the same thing.

The difference between an *avatar*, as Hindus say, and the incarnation, as Christians say, is nowhere more apparent than when Hindus learn about the death of Jesus on the cross. In Mark's Gospel, for example, Jesus dies a very un-Krishna-like death, deserted by his disciples, in agony and despairing that even God has abandoned him. Vishnu's *avatar*s do not die in despair. They are divine and not subject to such human fragility. The God Christians know is a God who has taken on our humanity so radically that dying in despair of God has paradoxically become part of the character of God. Hinduism is different. Sometimes this difference will be wonderfully enlightening for Christians struggling to understand their own faith. Other times, this difference will be profoundly perplexing.

However, Rama, another *avatar* of Vishnu, is a real human being. What might this mean for Hindus interested in the Christian doctrine of the incarnation? Hindus can practice comparative theology as well. As with Christians doing their theology comparatively, this may require Hindus to begin asking questions that they have not asked before. In this case, the discussion may very well turn out to be as exciting for Christians as it is for Hindus.

The Meaning of Death in Buddhism and Christianity

The first exercise in doing theology comparatively involved using a Hindu story to understand a familiar parable of Jesus in new ways. The second exercise has to do with Christianity's understanding of death and resurrection.

The reality of death is a basic concern for all human beings. Not surprisingly, the meaning of death and its relationship to life are of central concern not only to Christians but to Buddhists as well. Dogen Zenshi (1200–1251 C.E.), one of the founders of Zen in Japan, once remarked: "The clarification of birth and death is the most important thing in Buddhist teaching."[4] Dogen was born into a family of minor aristocrats and was orphaned by age seven. As a teenager, he became a Buddhist monk at one of the largest monasteries in Japan. Gradually, however, he became so discouraged with his religious life that he left his monastery and journeyed to China, where he began to practice Zen.

After attaining enlightenment in China, Dogen returned to Japan to become the founder of the Soto School of Zen. Today he is recognized around the world as one of the great creative minds of the Buddhist tradition. Over some twenty-two years, Dogen gave a series of lectures and sermons that were eventually collected into a volume known as the *Shôbôgenzô*, the "Eye and Treasury of the True Law." One of its chapters, entitled "*Shôji*," is a short essay on the relationship between life and death.

In this essay, Dogen notes that for those who are not yet enlightened, life is lived under the specter of death. A life lived constantly aware of an inevitable death is a life diminished by fear and driven by anxiety. For the enlightened, on the other hand, human existence is a continuous process of coming into life and dying. Birth and death are not experienced as two events separated by years of time. For the enlightened, time is an eternal present where the moment of birth and the moment of death are not two different moments. Continually we come into existence and pass out of existence, we are born and we die moment by moment. For this reason, life should not be thought of as the opposite of death. Life and death are not two different things. The enlightened mind does not see life and death in endless antagonism.

Therefore, Dogen thinks of enlightenment as clinging neither to life nor to death individually either. Clinging to life or to death is living life anxiously and obsessively, longing for death and despising life or grasping life desperately and cursing death.

> It is a mistake to think that life changes to death....when life comes, accept it as it is; when death comes, accept it as it is. Do not hate or desire either one.[5]

The one who thinks of death as a dreadful event looming before him in the future also sees life as that which is inevitably slipping away. This person is alienated from death (for it is the enemy of life) but is also alienated from life (for it has become something other than ourselves to which we cling in desperation).

Buddhism does not strive for the banishment of death from life. Buddhists do not seek an immortality beyond death because death is not seen as something alien to life or an enemy to be overcome. Instead, the

147

point of Buddhist religious practice is to see life and death as they truly
are in themselves, not as they appear to the unenlightened mind. The unenlightened mind sees death as a terror to be feared and therefore clings
to life anxiously. The enlightened mind does not see death and life pit-
ted against each other as two separate events, but rather life and death in
their "suchness." When Buddhists, especially Zen Buddhists, speak of
the suchness of things, they mean the original naturalness of things before the distortions of the unenlightened mind, the mind that clings and
is driven by anxiety, are imposed on them. When death is no longer
looked on as the opposite of life and life the opposite of death, then life
and death are freed from the distortions of our anxious, obsessive ego to
be what they are in themselves, their "suchness."

In the Shôbôgenzô, Dogen calls this "not-two-ness" of life and
death shôji, or "life/death," because they are but two aspects of the same,
unified reality. Enlightenment means that the nonduality of life and
death has become for us a principle of our daily lives. The enlightened
mind is driven neither by a fear of death nor by an obsession with life.

> Life and death [shôji] itself is the life of Buddha. If you despise
> and reject it you lose the life of the Buddha. Consequently, when
> you are attached to life and death you also lose the life of Buddha
> and are left with only his outer form. Only when you do not hate
> life and death or desire nirvana will you enter the mind of
> Buddha. Do not try to define it with your mind or describe it with
> words.[6]

When Dogen speaks of the "life of the Buddha," he means the enlightened mind that, like the Buddha, is free from attachment to life and death.
To "despise and reject" either life or death means dealing with the world
and ourselves with a mind that is distorted by illusions. Curiously, Dogen
advises us not only to abandon our hatred of life and death but also to stop
desiring Nirvana. The unenlightened mind thinks of Nirvana as an escape
from this world of life and death. Nirvana desired as an escape is not true
Nirvana. When Nirvana is seen as identical with this world of life and
death, an escape no longer desired, then Nirvana becomes the suchness
of life and death. Therefore, Dogen is saying that enlightenment is not a
matter of escaping our real situation into a false Nirvana that is beyond

both life and death. Instead, enlightenment has to do with embracing both life and death as they really are for us here and now.

> Trying to find Buddha outside the world of life and death is like pointing your cart north when you want to go south or facing south to look for the Ursa Major [in the northern sky]. If you do this you will lose the way of liberation.[7]

Only a fool would look for the Big Dipper (Ursa Major) in the south. Only the deluded look for enlightenment in a Nirvana that is separate from the ordinary reality of living and dying.

External Life or Life/Death?

Professor Masao Abe, one of the great exponents of Zen Buddhist thought today, offers his own interpretation of Dogen's understanding of shôji. According to Abe,

> ...living as it is, is no more than dying, and at the same time there is no living separate from dying. This means that life itself is death and death itself is life. That is, we do not shift sequentially from birth to death, but undergo living-dying in each and every moment.[8]

Enlightenment is being obsessed with neither life nor death. Enlightenment means realizing concretely that we are coming into life and dying every moment. Buddhism teaches that we must awaken to this truth of our existence experientially from within. Thus, according to Abe, awakening to shôji does not mean living 50 percent and dying 50 percent. By awakening to shôji, we finally begin to live 100 percent and die 100 percent. Only by being fully alive are we able to embrace the reality of death fully. Only by being fully dead are we able to embrace the reality of life fully.[9]

The Buddhist understanding of life and death, in Abe's view, is very different from Christianity's understanding. In pointing out these differences, Abe becomes an insightful critic of Christianity. For example, Abe notes that Christianity does not understand human existence as a continuous living and dying as Zen Buddhism does. Christianity assumes that life and death are opposites. Life must inevitably submit to death as the enemy of life. Therefore, Christianity looks for the conquest of death in the victory of God's eternal life over death. In contrast, Zen seeks enlightenment by awakening to the nonduality of life and death (*shôji*). Whereas Christianity asks us to hope in a resurrection into eternal life where death has been vanquished, Buddhism teaches us to awaken to the truth of our continuous living and dying moment by moment.[10]

Is Masao Abe correct about Christianity? Does Christianity make a sharp distinction between life and death and then teach us to hope in the victory of life over death? What do Christians believe about the relationship between life and death? Certainly Christianity does see salvation as the victory of God's eternal life over the power that death holds over us. In the Letter to the Hebrews in the New Testament, we are assured that Jesus Christ has defeated the prince of death in order to "free those who through fear of death had been subject to slavery all their life." (Heb 2:15). In this passage, life and death are conceived of as mutual enemies.

The roots of this Christian teaching can be seen in Paul's interpretation of the story of the first sin of Adam in the Garden of Eden. In Paul's reading of the Genesis story, human beings were created by God to enjoy life in abundance. Because of the sin of Adam, however, all creation has now become subject to the "slavery to corruption" (Rm 8:21). Death has entered the world because of sin. This means that death, the enemy of life, is not the work of God. Death enters into human history subsequent to creation as a result of Adam's rebellion against God's original plan (Rm 5:12). Our original intimacy with the source of life, the creator, has been cut off. Now we live anxious lives under the reign of death. Therefore, death is not natural, not intended by God, but rather is a punishment for our rebellion against God, the "wages of sin" (Rm 6:23).

In keeping with his view of death as a result of our sinfulness, Paul thinks of salvation as our deliverance from the power of death as the gift of eternal life. The redemption of our bodies that has been secured by Christ is a victory over the reign of death. This means that the death and resurrection of Jesus Christ are decisive for Paul. Through

Jesus' rising from the dead, death's long reign over human life is ended. "The wages of sin is death, but the gift of God is eternal life in Christ Jesus our Lord" (Rm 6:23).

Consequently, on the relationship of life and death, Buddhism and Christianity would seem to be very different. For Dogen, ultimately there is no dualism of life and death and so no victory of life over death. Enlightenment is the continual arising of *shôji*, the nonduality of life and death, moment by moment. Buddhists do not look for an ultimate victory of life over death and do not seek the banishment of death from our lives by the power of God to resurrect life out of death. Rather, Buddhists seek to awaken to the reality of life and death in their "suchness," apart from our fear of death and our clinging to life in order to be liberated from our obsession with both. To be liberated from our preoccupations with life means that we are finally free to embrace death. To be liberated from our obsession with death means that we are finally free to embrace life.

The Resurrection of the Dead

In doing theology comparatively, Christians try to understand their faith in new ways by using the teachings of other religions as a resource. Now that we have looked at Dogen's understanding of death on its own terms and noted some real differences between the Buddhist and the Christian understanding of the relationship between life and death, we are in a position to see if Dogen's religious teachings might serve as a resource for understanding Christianity more deeply. Can Dogen's *shôji* serve as a tool for exploring Christianity's understanding of death and the meaning of Christian faith in the resurrection?

Christianity's religious hope is centered on the victory of life over death. In this respect, Abe's understanding of Christianity is correct. But I would hasten to add that this victory of eternal life over death does not entail a denial of death. The victory of life over death envisioned by Christian faith is a transformation of our lives that requires us, but also empowers us, to enter into death with faith and hope. Christianity rejects any understanding of resurrection that does not lead first to the cross and the tomb. Furthermore, for Christians, the resurrection does not mean escaping the biological necessity of dying. All human bodies will one day return to dust. Faith in the resurrection of the body does not make Christian believers exempt from the reality of the body's physical demise. In fact, if Christ's death and resurrection are the model, then the resurrection Christians seek requires them to embrace death radically. The ultimate meaning of life, the new life of the resurrection, is revealed only to those who have embraced the cross of Jesus. We rise with Christ to newness of life only after first dying with Christ. Those who refuse to die to their sinful selves will never know the new life that is the resurrection. For this reason, Christianity stands against all forms of pop psychology and spiritual "quick fixes" that promise easy paths to immortality by denying the reality of death.

Normally, Christians think of the resurrection from the dead as a saving event that awaits them in the future and not as a present reality. God will not abandon us to the abyss, but will raise us up to newness of life with him in heaven. According to the apostle Paul,

> [I wish] to know [Christ] and the power of his resurrection and [the] sharing of his sufferings by being conformed to his death, if somehow I may attain the resurrection from the dead. It is not that I have already taken hold of it or have already attained perfect maturity, but I continue my pursuit in hope that I may possess it, since I have indeed been taken possession of by Christ [Jesus]. (Phil 3:10–12)

In fact, a search of the New Testament produces passages that condemn the belief that the resurrection from the dead is a present reality. For example, in the Second Letter to Timothy, belief in the resurrection as a present reality is rejected as "idle talk" that has "deviated from the truth" (2 Tim 2:16–18).

Despite the general tendency for Christians to think of the resurrection as a future event awaiting them only after their biological death, there is also strong support in the New Testament for the belief that the resurrection is a present reality that has begun here and now in our bodies. The notion of the resurrection as a present reality is especially evident where the New Testament discusses the meaning of baptism for

152

Christians. Generally, Paul wrote about baptism as an incorporation into the death of Jesus Christ here and now and the beginning of a hope in a future resurrection. However, in the letters to the Colossians and the Ephesians, which may have been written by Paul very late in life or by his disciples after his death, incorporation into the death of Christ through baptism also means rising with Christ here and now, in this very body.

> You were buried with him in baptism, in which you were also raised
> with him through faith in the power of God, who raised him from
> the dead. (Col 2:12)

> If then you were raised with Christ, seek what is above, where Christ
> is seated at the right hand of God. Think of what is above, not of
> what is on earth. For you have died, and your life is hidden with
> Christ in God. (Col 3:1–4)

> But God, who is rich in mercy, because of the great love he had for
> us, even when we were dead in our transgressions, brought us to life
> with Christ (by grace you have been saved), raised us up with him,
> and seated us with him in the heavens in Christ Jesus... (Eph 2:4–6)

Baptism is not merely a ceremony signifying admission into a social group. Baptism entails a radical transformation of the believer, a dying with Christ and rising with him into a new kind of existence here on earth. Neither is baptism only a token of a future salvation. In the dying and rising of baptism, the church witnesses to the beginning of eternal life here and now in the baptized.

The resurrection from the dead is, in part, a future hope for Christians in which God's eternal life will be victorious over death. In this respect, life and death are seen as adversaries. Death menaces life. Through God's redeeming grace, life is triumphant over death. In this respect, Abe is correct. Christianity and Buddhism have very different conceptions of the relationship between life and death. The totality of Christian faith, however, is more complex than this. Christianity also sees the resurrection as a present reality, a radical spiritual transformation that takes place here and now. In rising with Christ, a new kind of existence begins for the believer, even before the coming of biological death.¹¹ With Dogen in mind, we should note that when Christians think of the resurrection as a future reality, as they usually do, life and death inevitably are seen as opposites. However, is this the case when the resurrection is seen as a present reality? From the perspective of a resurrection already fully realized, how should Christians think of the relationship between life and death? What if we read these New Testament passages that speak of the resurrection as a present reality with Dogen's notion of the nonduality of life and death (*shôji*) in mind? Doing so will lead us to reflect more deeply on the fact that the meaning of biological death has been transformed for Christian believers by the resurrection of Christ.

The Meaning of Death in Light of the Resurrection

How does the reality of the resurrection from the dead transform our understanding of the meaning of biological death? In Paul's view, death has come into the world as punishment for sin. In the Garden of Eden, Adam and Eve were not subject to the penalty of death until after falling into sin (Rm 5:12–14; 1 Cor 15:21–22). Therefore, in Paul's theology, death must be seen as the "wages of sin" (Rm 6:23), and not a simple biological fact. At times, Paul speaks of death as a power "law" (Rm 8:2) which "reigns" over sinful human beings (Rm 5:14,17, 21) and as an "enemy" (1 Cor 15:26). But by dying with Christ through baptism, death has lost its power over us (Rm 6:1–11).

When the resurrection is thought of as a future event, life yearns to be liberated from all that would diminish it and, indeed, "the last enemy to be destroyed is death" (1 Cor. 15:26). But when the resurrection is experienced as a reality already present here and now, then we must say that human existence has been transformed even though biological death remains. If this is the case, then the meaning of biological death must be changed for a Christian believer who has been transformed by the power of the resurrection. For those living the old life of sin and futility, death remains a dreadful foe, the last enemy. For those who have risen with Christ, however, death has lost its "sting" (1 Cor 15:55). Therefore, Christians need to distinguish between two kinds of death. On the one hand, there is death as the "wages of sin" and a power threatening our sinful, egocentric lives. On the other hand, there is death as a simple biological fact, a natural part of life that exists even after the radical transformation of our existence in the resurrection.

How might Christians understand the meaning of biological death from the perspective of a resurrection from the dead realized in the present? If eternal life has begun already for us, how has the relationship between biological life and biological death been transformed? Dogen's notion of *shôji*, the "not-two-ness" of life and death, might serve as a model for Christians who want to understand their own belief in the resurrection of the body more deeply.

Buddhism thinks of the enlightened mind as one that clings to neither life nor death but rather realizes life, just as it is, and death, just as it is, in their suchness, apart from our obsessions with them. For the unenlightened, according to Dogen, life is lived under the specter of inevitable death. For the enlightened, however, human existence is a continuous living and dying, where life can be fully lived because death has not been denied and where death can be embraced because life has been fully lived.

Christians do not speak of the suchness of life and death, but rather of becoming a "new creation" by dying and rising with Christ. Paul writes, "so whoever is in Christ, is a new creation: the old things have passed away; behold, new things have come" (2 Cor 5:17). Using Dogen's notion of the nonduality of life and death (*shôji*) as a guide, we might say that becoming a new creation in the resurrection entails a continuous embracing of death as the concrete form of being fully alive (fully resurrected) in Christ. Only by dying with Christ day by day, moment by moment, does eternal life in Christ become a reality for us here and now. When the resurrection is thought of as a present reality, Christians must recognize, along with Buddhists, that human existence has been transformed into a continuous living and dying, what Dogen calls *shôji*, what Christianity calls "dying and rising with Christ."

This would mean that in becoming a "new creation in Christ" in the resurrection, Christians recognize that life and death are no longer opposed to one another as enemies. Through our dying and rising with Christ here and now, our sins have been forgiven and we are no longer subject to the dominion of death. Death is no longer a power that rules over our lives to diminish and distort our humanity. Rather, death is a creation of God, which, like all aspects of God's creation, should be accepted in gratitude for the grace that it is. Life is a gift from God, and so is death. Christians can welcome this truth only from within the transformation of life and death that is the resurrection.

Ars Moriendi: *Dying as Spiritual "Practice"*

Dogen's understanding of life and death opens up other truths concerned with the resurrection for Christians to ponder. For example, Dogen thinks of enlightenment as the continual "practice" of *shôji*. When Dogen speaks of *shôji* as a form of practice, he means that the nonduality of life and death is realized concretely in every aspect of our lives moment by moment. In other words, enlightenment is not a strange mystical state of consciousness that takes the mind into a realm far removed from the world that unenlightened people inhabit. According to Dogen, the enlightened mind arises moment by moment in the daily course of our normal activities. In thinking of *shôji* as a form of "practice," Dogen is saying that the nonduality of life and death is a Buddhist form of asceticism. Enlightenment means making concrete the nonantagonism, the "not-two-ness" of life and death as we go about our everyday life.

I believe something similar can be said about Christianity's experience of faith in the resurrection. As a present reality, the resurrection's reconciliation of life and death must be a form of asceticism. For example, consider the following passage from the writings of Paul.

[We are] always carrying about in the body the dying of Jesus, so that the life of Jesus may also be manifested in our body. For we who live are constantly being given up to death for the sake of Jesus, so that the life of Jesus may be manifested in our mortal flesh. (2 Cor 4:10–11)

How does Dogen's notion of *shôji* as "practice" allow Christians to understand this passage in new ways? Normally, biblical scholars think of this passage in terms of Paul's view of the resurrection as a future event awaiting us after death. Paul's understanding of our resurrection from the dead, however, may not be as clear as we sometimes think. Dogen's Zen perspective on life and death should lead Christians to be attentive to the fact that Paul thinks of our relationship with Jesus' death and his new life in terms of embodiment. To the extent that "we...are constantly being given up to death for the sake of Jesus," the life of Jesus is being revealed in our bodies. Paul thinks of the body as the place where Jesus' new life is manifest in terms of the Lord's dying, or in Dogen's terms, the place where the nonduality of life and death arise within the world. According to Paul, the embodiment of Jesus' life and death goes on "constantly." In the ordinary events of our daily lives, the resurrected Christ is "manifested in our mortal flesh." For Christians, the resurrected life is a form of what Buddhists call "practice" or what Christians know more familiarly as a spiritual exercise.

Dogen's view of *shôji* as practice also leads Christians to rethink their medieval spiritual notion of the *ars moriendi*, the "art of dying." When the medieval monks talked about dying as an "art," they were not talking about a longing to escape this world and its demands. Dying was considered an "art" because the contemplation of death led to a deeper and more concrete awareness of being alive. The contemplation of death was not intended to lead one away from this world, but rather to help one to live in this world as God's creature, not as an anxious sinner driven by guilt to despise life and curse death. Masao Abe's interpretation of Dogen is helpful in understanding the *ars moriendi* using Buddhist thought as a resource. Recall that, according to Abe, Dogen does not think of *shôji* as being 50 percent alive and 50 percent dead. Rather, only by being completely alive can we completely embrace death. Only by completely embracing death can we finally become completely alive. For Christians, the "art of dying" is a spiritual "practice" that does not entail an escape from this world. By practicing death as an art, we come to embody in our concrete lives the new life of the resurrection here and now. An oft-quoted passage from Paul comes readily to mind here: "Yet I live, no longer I, but Christ lives in me" (Gal 2:20). For Buddhists, dying is a form of practice. For Christians it is an "art"—if death and life are understood nondualistically. Christians should think of the resurrection not only as a transformation of the meaning of death but also as a transformation of the meaning of life. Because the meaning of death has been transformed in Christ, we are no longer afraid to be alive. Fully alive in Christ, we can fully open ourselves to the reality of our biological death as the creature God originally created us to be. In the resurrection we have become a new creation. Death and life are no longer at war within us. In embracing the cross of Christ, the real meaning of life becomes real and concrete in our very bodies.

The Pluralist Question

A pluralist theologian might want to suggest that when Dogen speaks of enlightenment and a Christian speaks of becoming a "new creation in Christ," they are in fact giving different names to the same reality. Are Dogen's "enlightened mind" and Paul's "new creation in Christ" different expressions of what John Hick calls "reality-centeredness" or what Paul Knitter calls "sōtéria" or what Stanley Samartha calls "Mystery"? As I have argued earlier in this book, a major problem with pluralist theologies is that they are too quick to focus on similarities and fail to pay sufficient attention to the theologically interesting differences that distinguish religions. For Christians who wish to do theology comparatively, differences can be as illuminating and as useful as the similarities that link religions.

Dogen's notion of the nonduality of life and death *(shôji)* has proven to be useful as a resource for helping Christians to reflect on the doctrine of the resurrection in new ways. As a model for understanding the resurrection, however, Dogen's notion of life/death eventually breaks down. Dying and rising with Christ means becoming a new creation, here and now. But at the same time, dying with Christ also means becoming heir to the resurrection as a future promise that will become real "on the last day." If the resurrection is thought of as an eschatological hope, Dogen's *shôji* and Christianity's resurrection seem very different indeed.

A passage from the Hebrew scriptures often read at Christian funerals is taken from the book of Job. After losing all that he held precious in his life, Job is accused of being a sinner and thus deserving of his plight. In response, Job declaims,

Oh, would that my words were written down!
Would that they were inscribed in a record:
That with an iron chisel and with lead
they were cut in the rock forever!
But as for me, I know that my Vindicator lives,
and that he will at last stand forth upon the dust;
Whom I myself shall see:
my own eyes, not another's, shall behold him,
And from my flesh I shall see God;
my inmost being is consumed with longing.

(Job 19:23–27)

Covered in woe, Job looks upon this world as a place of desolation and sorrow. His alienation from his present life leads him to place all his hope in a future vindication. For Job, redemption is not a matter of awakening to the suchness of life and death as Dogen counsels. Christianity's eschatological hope points to a redemption *from* this world which will come some time in the future. Instead of realizing life and death in their suchness, Christian hope reflects a profound alienation from the present state of life and a longing for what can come to pass only through the grace of God, who has promised to bring eternal life out of death. Christian hope in a future resurrection is proclaimed in the moral condemnations of the prophets and heard in the cry of the poor. Eschatological hope is a kind of openness to reality, but not in the Buddhist sense of the suchness of all. Instead, Christian hope in the resurrection to come leads believers to an openness to the world as it is being transformed by God in fulfillment of his promise.

Therefore, a full interpretation of the Christian notion of life and death must preserve within itself a tension between the reality of the resurrection as present here and now, on the one hand, and at the same time the reality of the resurrection as a future event and eschatological hope. Neither side of this tension can replace the other without thereby losing something essential to the Christian religious vision. Buddhism does not recognize the religious meaning of Christianity's eschatological hope in a future resurrection from the dead. In fact, I think that most Buddhists would see eschatological hope in the resurrection as yet another form of desire or obsession that must be renounced in order to become enlightened. But here, of course, Buddhists must speak for

159

their own tradition and Christians should listen attentively. I can only presume that hearing Buddhists speak at some length on this issue would be very instructive to Christians who wish to plumb even deeper into the depth of the meaning of the resurrection.

*   *   *

In the first exercise in comparative theology, the story of Krishna and the milkmaids proved to be a useful tool for opening up the familiar story of the Prodigal Son for Christians to read in new ways. The same can be said of Dogen's *shôji*, the nonduality of life and death. This Buddhist teaching can be a resource for Christians seeking to explore the full meaning of the resurrection. As exercises in comparative theology, neither of these two attempts to do theology comparatively started with the presumption that all religions are attempts to name the same transcendent reality, as with pluralist theologies of religion, or that non-Christian religions all reveal the mystery of Christ in their depths, as with Rahner's inclusivist theology of religion, or that non-Christian religions are merely human creations, as with Barth's exclusivist theology. Instead, the two experiments in comparative theology began with what non-Christians actually believe and then went on to reflect on these beliefs in a way that proved helpful for Christians trying to understanding themselves in relationship to their non-Christian neighbors.

Now we need to ask more specifically how comparative theology offers an alternative to the theology of religions today and how comparative theology might serve as a practical way for Christians and their neighbors who follow different religious paths to live with one another responsibly and creatively.

NOTES

1. The most important scriptural source for the many stories regarding Krishna is the *Bhagavata Purana*. For a very helpful discussion of Krishna and the *Bhagavata Purana*, see the essays collected in *Krishna: Myths, Rites and Attitudes*, ed. Milton Singer (Chicago: University of Chicago Press, 1966).

2. *Bhagavata Purana* X, 29, 8. See also *Krishna*, ed. Singer, 154–55.

3. See Diana Eck's comments on this story in *Encountering God: A Spiritual Journey from Bozeman to Banaras* (Boston: Beacon Press, 1993), 45–46.

4. See Masao Abe, *A Study of Dogen*, ed. Steve Heine (Albany, N.Y.: SUNY Press, 1992), 173.

5. Dogen, "Shoji," in *Shôbôgenzô*, trans. Kosen Nisiyama and John Stevens (Sendai, Japan: Daihokkaikaku Publishing Co., 1975), 21.

6. Ibid., 21–22.

7. Ibid., 21.

8. Abe, *A Study of Dogen* (Albany, N.Y.: SUNY Press, 1992), 170–71.

9. Ibid.

10. For Abe's criticism of Christianity, see Abe, *A Study of Dogen*, 170–72.

11. See for example, the *Catechism of the Catholic Church* #1002: "Christ will raise us up 'on the last day'; but it is also true that, in a certain way, we have already risen with Christ. For, by virtue of the Holy Spirit, Christian life is already now on earth a participation in the death and Resurrection of Christ."

Chapter 8

AFTER PLURALISM:
DOING THEOLOGY COMPARATIVELY

The great scholar of Buddhism Edward Conze once picked up a copy of *Butler's Lives of the Saints* to learn about what Christians think of as an ideal religious life. He later remarked that, in *Butler's*, he failed to find even one Christian saint whom a Buddhist could admire. Commenting on Conze's statement, Joseph Dinoia observes that this does not indicate that Christian saints are despicable frauds, but only that what Buddhists see as greatness in a religious figure differs significantly from what Christians see as greatness. The differences that distinguish religions from one another are sizable. Does this mean that believers from different religious traditions have nothing to learn from one another? I hope that the two examples of doing Christian theology offered in the previous chapter have proven that Christians can learn a great deal from other religious traditions.

In this chapter I plan to reflect on these two examples of comparative theology. I hope to demonstrate that the best way for Christians to respond to the fact of religious diversity today lies in doing theology comparatively. By exploring the truths of Christianity in dialogue with the teachings and traditions of other religious believers, Christians will come to embrace their own cherished beliefs in new ways. In the process, Christianity will be enriched and Christians will forge bonds of respect and even admiration with their non-Christian neighbors.

Responsibility and Creativity

Discussions among Christians about the theology of religions have been lively and provocative. Now, however, the time has come to recognize that the debate between exclusivists, inclusivists, and pluralists has reached an impasse. From its opening pages, this book has been written out of the conviction that today Christians need to develop skills for living responsibly and creatively with non-Christian believers. Measured by this standard, the basic options for a theology of religions, including the pluralist option, are inadequate to the needs of Christians today.

When I say we need to develop "skills for living responsibly with non-Christian believers," I want to draw attention to the fact that theologies of religion, including pluralist theologies, can easily become a sophisticated way to avoid dealing with the moral, theological, and spiritual challenges that non-Christian religions pose to Christian believers today. The great religions of the world, including Christianity of course, cannot be reduced to variant expressions of the Golden Rule or differing interpretations of the same ultimate reality. They differ from one another in ways of great religious importance and theological interest. Claiming otherwise does violence to the specific character of the different religious traditions. The differences that distinguish religions need to be recognized and respected. Buddhists, for example, should not be required to polish out the aspects of the Dharma that are the most difficult for Christians to accept in the name of "being open." The aspects of the Dharma that differ most starkly from the Gospels may constitute the most valuable truths Buddhists have to teach Christians. The same courtesy should be extended to all the other religions, including Christianity. Christian believers should not be required to reformulate their beliefs in compliance with the demand that their beliefs become acceptable to all other religious believers, as suggested by Wilfred Cantwell Smith. Living responsibly with non-Christian believers means living with non-Christians in a way that is true to what is most basic and most demanding about the Christian tradition. As a Christian who regularly gathers with Buddhist friends to learn from them the wisdom of the Dharma, I am not at all interested in hearing a version of Buddhism watered down for Christian consumption or presented with the presupposition that Buddhism and Christianity are really saying the same thing. My Buddhist friends expect nothing less when they ask me about my own Christian religious tradition.

For example, the story of Krishna and the *gopis* was seen to be a helpful way for Christians to reflect on the reality of divine love in their lives. Yet in Hindu tradition, Krishna is seen as an *avatar* (divine descent) of Vishnu, one of the great divinities of India, not the incarnation of the Word, as with Jesus in Christian tradition. Jesus cannot be made into an *avatar* of Vishnu without distortion. Christians should not think of Krishna as the Word made flesh, for this too is a distortion. To confuse the notion of *avatar* and an incarnation in order to seem tolerant or open-minded is misguided and irresponsible to both Hinduism and Christianity.

When I say that Christians need "skills for living creatively with non-Christian believers," I want to draw attention to the fact that a theology of religions can become a sophisticated way to refuse to take advantage of what I take to be an enormous opportunity for Christians today: the chance to learn from their non-Christian neighbors. If a theology of religions can become a way to avoid dealing with the moral, intellectual, and spiritual demands religions make, so also it can act as a mask for a subtle form of religious intolerance. If we should believe that all religions are ultimately saying the same thing or responding to the same ultimate reality, then there is nothing a Buddhist or a Confucian or a Muslim could say that would require me, as a Christian, to change my mind, at least regarding matters of great theological importance. A Confucian has her own way of talking about Ultimate Reality and I have my own. Non-Christians, however, teach things of fundamental importance that Christians do not teach. I think Christians should listen to what their non-Christian neighbors are saying, take it seriously, and find ways to respond to non-Christians creatively.

Failing to take the teaching of other religious traditions seriously is intolerance, although certainly a subtle form of intolerance. None of the theologians associated with the theology of religions is calling for intolerance. The pluralist theologians, especially, can be singled out for their great concern to promote religious tolerance through their pluralist approach to religious diversity. Their motives, in this respect, are beyond reproach. Pluralist theologies, however, are not particularly helpful in empowering Christians to engage their non-Christian neighbors creatively.

For example, Dogen's understanding of life and death proved to be helpful in opening up for Christians deeper truths having to do with the doctrine of the resurrection. Normally Christians think of the resurrection as a future hope in the triumph of God's eternal life over the power of death. By taking Dogen's Zen Buddhist teaching on life and death seriously, we were required and also enabled to look at Christian beliefs in new ways. Buddhist wisdom became a resource for Christians seeking to understand themselves and their beliefs in light of the traditions of their Buddhist neighbors. Christians who look on Dogen as a source of inspiration and insight will look on their Buddhist neighbors differently than Christians who know nothing of Buddhism. This is a creative response to the fact of religious diversity.

An Alternative to the Theology of Religions

Today the controversy over pluralist theologies is given a great deal of attention. Less noticed but more deserving of our attention is a small group of Christian theologians who are beginning to explore the truths of Christianity by comparing their faith with the faith of their non-Christian neighbors. These comparative theologians, and not the pluralists, will be decisive in the future. Donald Mitchell, for example, is exploring Christian spirituality using Zen Buddhism from Japan. John Cobb, Leo Lefebure, and John Keenan are asking new questions about the meaning of Christ using Buddhist thought. Francis X. Clooney and David Carpenter are exploring Christianity by comparing Christian texts with Hindu texts. John Berthrong is a Christian theologian who is learning from Confucianism. David Burrell studies Islamic thought in order to deepen his understanding of the Christian doctrine of God.[1] These theologians are not particularly interested in the question of a theology of religions. Instead, they are exploring their own Christian faith in dialogue with another religious tradition.

At this time in the history of Christianity, as Christian believers look beyond their own faith into a world of immense religious diversity, a completely satisfactory account of the meaning of non-Christian religions is no longer possible. Our survey of the debate over the theology of religions amply supports this conclusion. None of the three basic candidates for a theology of religions meets the standards set by the two criteria we have been discussing. This being the case, the question of a theology of religions should be put aside for the time being. Abandoning the quest for a theology of religions will seem outrageous to some. However, honesty to our historical situation requires that we look for new ways to respond to the diversity of religions today.

There are two basic reasons why a completely satisfactory theology of religions is not possible. First, we know too much about non-Christian believers and their religious traditions today. A Christian cannot say that a Muslim is "Godless" because she does not look upon Jesus as the divine savior of the world. Even a short visit to a mosque, for example, should impress upon a Christian the intensity with which Muslims believe in the oneness and majesty of God and the ethical demands that flow from this belief. The more Christians actually know about their Muslim neighbors, the less satisfactory exclusivist theologies of religions become. Similarly, there may be a very solid basis in Christian doctrine for Christians to believe that when Buddhists speak of "emptiness," they are speaking imperfectly of the same Mystery that Christians know as the God of Jesus Christ, as inclusivist and pluralist theologies hold in their different ways. The more Christians study Buddhism, however, the more they will come to appreciate that, in some ways at least, Buddhism is far more different than they ever imagined. Exclusivism, inclusivism, and pluralism become less and less plausible the more we find out about the actual beliefs of our non-Christian neighbors.

The second reason a completely satisfactory theology of religions is not possible today has to do with the need Christians have to learn from other religious believers. Today Christians need a way to explore their own faith more aware of the beliefs of their non-Christian neighbors. In our schools, Muslim children refrain from eating lunch during Ramadan and may want to pray to Allah, the merciful, the beneficent, during the school day, in conformity with the command to pray in the Five Pillars of Islam. In those same schools, Buddhist children may be asked to show how they pray to the Buddha. In this case, we are in for a surprise. Buddhists do not pray to the Buddha.

Buddhists do not think of the Buddha as a god. This surprise should be seen as a learning opportunity for all involved. As we have seen, a problem that taints all three options for a theology of religions is that they can be used to inoculate Christians against the power and novelty of other religious traditions.[2] Exclusivist theologians, like Karl Barth, see non-Christian religions as entirely different and of no consequence for Christian believers. Inclusivist theologians like Karl Rahner and pluralist theologians see non-Christian religions as fundamentally similar to Christianity. Thus, inclusivist and pluralist theologies can have the unintended effect of rendering the differences that distinguish other religions from Christianity less interesting to Christians.

A complete and satisfactory theology of religions is not possible right now. I make this claim not to promote a kind of agnosticism about the meaning of the diversity of religions for Christian believers. Instead, I want to point Christians in the direction of a more creative way for responding to religious diversity today. The two experiments in comparative theology offered in the preceding chapter were attempts to understand the meaning of Christianity using the teachings of other religious traditions. By comparing their own faith with the faith of other religious believers, Christians can deepen their own religious lives and come to a better understanding of the gospel. And in the very process of doing this, Christians will also come to a deeper knowledge and appreciation of believers who follow other religious paths. Thus, by exploring the meaning of their own faith by doing theology in dialogue with their non-Christian neighbors, Christians will have developed practical skills for living responsibly and creatively with non-Christians.

Comparative theology is a way for Christians to respond to religious diversity but is not another candidate for a theology of religions. Unlike theologies of religions, comparative theology does not start with a grand theory of religion in general that claims to account for all religions. Therefore the two exercises in doing theology comparatively in the last chapter did not begin from a perspective beyond all the actual religions such as John Hick's "Real," Paul Knitter's *sōtéria*, Wilfred Cantwell Smith's "transcendence," or Stanley Samartha's "Mystery." Comparative theology is done by Christian believers in the hope of deepening their understanding of Christianity. Therefore comparative theology does not look for some abstract lowest common denominator or essence that all religions, including Christianity, share. Instead of theories about religion in general, comparative theologians are interested in studying other religions on their own terms and then exploring their own Christian faith using what they have learned about the other religions.

Take the reflection in the preceding chapter on the meaning of death for Dogen, the Zen Buddhist. The theology of religions asks if the "suchness" that forms the standpoint of the enlightened mind for Dogen is in fact a Buddhist way of talking about what Christians mean when they say God. Comparative theology, in contrast, asks how Christians might deepen their own understanding of death in light of the resurrection using Dogen as a resource. In the process, Christians actually had to learn something about Zen Buddhism on its own terms, study it seriously and then return to their own tradition to reflect on its meaning in new and hopefully creative ways. This exercise in comparative theology did not begin with the theological presupposition that Zen Buddhism is merely a human creation that has nothing to do with Christian theology (Barth) or that Christians would find Christ revealed in the depths of Dogen's Zen doctrine (Rahner), or that Christianity and Zen are both trying to name the same Ultimate Reality (the pluralist theologians).

The same point can be made about the comparison of Krishna and the *gopis* with the parable of the Prodigal Son. The theology of religions asks if Vishnu (who appears to the *gopis* as Krishna) is in fact the same God who is worshiped by Christians. Comparative theology, in contrast, asks how Christians might deepen their own understanding of the parable of the Prodigal Son in light of this Hindu story. Hindu insight into divine love can become a resource for Christians in deepening their own spiritual lives. In order for this to happen, however, Christians had to learn about Hindus and take their stories seriously. In the process, both similarities and differences with Christian belief came to light. Not only the similarities but the differences as well turned out to be helpful for Christians in exploring their own beliefs. In addition, both the similarities and the differences are helpful in leading Christians and Hindus to live with one another responsibly and creatively.

Living with Tension

Thinking about Christian faith using a Hindu story about divine love and a Buddhist understanding of death means that we have begun to do theology comparatively. To be sure, these exercises entailed a careful study of a small part of Hinduism and Buddhism, but the real goal of the exercises was to gain a better understanding of the meaning of Christianity. Both exercises in comparative theology combined a study of non-Christian religions and a commitment to discovering more about the meaning of Christian faith. These two aspects of comparative theology form a tension. There is always a commitment to the Christian tradition, but at the same time, there must be an openness to the truths of non-Christian religions. On the one hand, comparative theology is Christian theology. Both of the exercises in the preceding chapter asked how Christians might understand their own faith more fully aware of the teachings and truths of other religious believers. On the other hand, comparative theology is a form of theology that requires Christians to go beyond their own religious tradition and expose themselves to teachings that may be strange, unsettling, or even disturbing. These two commitments are always in some form of tension when theology is done comparatively.

For example, the two exercises in the preceding chapter began with a study of what Hindus actually believe about their beloved Krishna and what Zen Buddhists think about death. Without a solid understanding of Hindu and Buddhist belief, the exercises would have been pointless. Comparative theology requires Christian believers to see non-Christian religions on their own terms, not as Christians want these religions to be in order to conform with Christian doctrine or a philosophical presupposition about religions in general. Therefore, in order to do comparative theology well, Christians must study non-Christian religions seriously. The beliefs of non-Christians must not be distorted in order to achieve a false harmony among faiths required by the assertion that all religions really reflect the same transcendent reality, as with pluralism. Neither should the beliefs of non-Christians be distorted in order to show that these beliefs have nothing to do with Christian revelation or that they are really talking about Christ and thus are anonymous Christians, as with exclusivism and inclusivism.

Thus, in doing theology comparatively, there will always be a tension between our commitments to the Christian tradition, on the one hand, and, on the other, to the allure of other religious traditions.[3] In order to understand Christianity in comparison with other religious traditions, we must resist the temptation to overcome this tension. Losing our commitment to the Christian tradition leads to the problem of relativism that sometimes troubles pluralist theologies of religions. Losing our sense of the allure of other religious traditions, however, is also disastrous for comparative theology, for this would mean that we, as Christian seekers, have cut ourselves off from the power of non-Christian religions to inspire new insights within us. The tension should not be lost. The real challenge is how to keep this tension creative.

This tension between commitment to Christianity and openness to other religious truths suggests that the best way to deal responsibly and creatively with religious diversity is to remain rooted in one's own religious tradition. By "remaining rooted" I do not mean closing ourselves off from the demanding and transforming truths of other religious traditions. This is the unhelpful legacy of exclusivist theologies. Rather, I am cautioning against adopting some meta-religious position that no actual religion holds. This is the danger courted by the pluralist approach to religious diversity. The pluralists ask us to move out of our own religious tradition (whether we be Christians or Confucians or otherwise) into a standpoint that no religion has taken for itself, in order to say that all religions are expressions or interpretations of the same transcendent Reality. Taking this meta-religious standpoint effectively destroys the tension in comparative theology between a commitment to a particular religious tradition and an openness to the truths of other religious traditions.

All the candidates for a theology of religions, not just the pluralist variety, to one extent or another lessen this tension. Barth's exclusivism seeks to inoculate the Christian believer from the often troubling truths of non-Christian religions by making a sharp distinction between revelation (something only Christians enjoy) and religion (something human beings have invented). There is no need for openness to other religious traditions. Christians are safely shielded from the tension between a commitment to Christian roots and an openness to other religious traditions. Rahner's inclusivist theology of religions lessens the tension as well. The roots in the Christian tradition are there, but the truths of non-Christian religions are rendered harmless from the beginning. No matter how different non-Christian religions may *seem*, in fact they are but lesser expressions of the same truths professed explicitly by Christianity. Rahner's problem is only exasperated in the candidates for a pluralist theology of religions. The Christian can be open to the truths of non-Christian religions because we can presume that all religions are expressions of the same transcendent truth. In making this move, the specific character of Christianity and the demands it places on believers are obscured. The tension between a real commitment to Christianity and a daring openness to another religious tradition is weakened, if not abandoned.

Beyond Tolerance

The deepest aspiration of comparative theology is a spiritual transformation of Christian believers. In this respect, the goal of comparative theology is the same as the goal of all Christian theology. Doing theology comparatively should have a concrete impact on the lives of Christian believers and the church as a whole. In addition, as a form of Christian theology, comparative theology should contribute to the common good of our society in general. In this respect, we need to take up a theme prominent in the works of the pluralist theologians, the need for religious tolerance today.

Diana Eck, who heads the Pluralism Project at Harvard University, has done a good job of mapping the shifting sands of religious diversity in the United States.[4] Religious diversity, of course, is nothing unique to the United States, although Eck notes that the United States may be the most religiously diverse society in the world.[5] Reflecting on her research, Eck points out that religious diversity is not a slogan like "multiculturalism," however important sensitivity to the variety of cultural perspectives may be as an ideal for Americans today. Religious diversity is already a fact that touches everyone. We ignore this fact at our own peril. Eck's research has led her to conclude that we must move beyond mere tolerance of religious diversity. Religious tolerance is a vital public virtue, to be sure, but too thin a foundation for the challenge facing American society today. Americans need to find ways of engaging diversity, or as I have said, of living creatively with religious diversity.

Let me note that, in addition to being a civic virtue, tolerance of religious paths not our own must be counted a theological virtue as well. Building on Eck's observation, let me say that religious tolerance is likewise too thin a foundation for Christianity as it seeks to respond to the challenge and opportunity posed by religious diversity to Christian believers. Christians can be tolerant of other religious traditions for any number of reasons. Karl Barth, who claimed that all religions were merely human inventions, nevertheless begins his discussion of non-Christian religions with a strong statement about the necessity of tolerance. Any discussion of non-Christians and their religions must be based first and last on tolerance, according to Barth. The tolerance of Christians, however, is not a matter of confusion about God's revelation. Rather, Christian tolerance is based in the forbearance that Christ himself shows in dealing with our refusal to believe.[6] Conversely, Rahner's inclusivist theology of the anonymous Christian leads Christian believers to tolerance as well. Non-Christians are to be respected because in the depths of their different religious traditions, the grace of the Holy Spirit is at work implicitly as it is at work explicitly in Christianity. A Christian pluralist can be tolerant of other religious traditions because she knows that all religious differences result from differing approaches to the same transcendent Reality. In none of these cases is tolerance based on a recognition of the religious and theological value of the real differences that distinguish the religions of the world from one another. Religious tolerance, however virtuous, does nothing to remove our ignorance of one another. Tolerance, of course, is obviously preferable to intolerance; yet the history of tolerance shows that it is perfectly happy with religious ghettos. We need to go beyond tolerance to a point where the differences between religions are seen as valuable opportunities for deepening our own religious commitments in conversation with other religious believers.

Diana Eck is right in concluding that we need to find ways to move beyond religious tolerance. Diversity not only needs to be tolerated but engaged energetically. We need a way to hold our most cherished beliefs and also our deepest religious differences not in isolation but in community with one another.[7] For Christian believers, this means that there is a need to develop new skills and cultivate personal qualities that will assist them in living well with their non-Christian neighbors. In this respect, I believe that doing theology comparatively has much to contribute. Comparative theology can be thought of as a skill very much needed today, a skill useful for taking advantage of the opportunities religious diversity presents to us today. Doing theology comparatively requires that Christians be directed outward in regard to religious diversity. Comparative theology helps to move us beyond religious tolerance in that it presumes that Christians should turn to Jews, Muslims, Buddhists, Hindus, and others in order to pursue their own religious quest.

In addition to being a skill useful for engaging religious diversity in a positive fashion today, I think that comparative theology is also helpful for cultivating personal qualities that we should recognize as virtues for a religiously diverse society such as ours. This leads us to the matter of friendships between believers from different religious traditions.

Interreligious Friendship

If Christians want to respond to religious diversity by doing theology comparatively, I suggest that they begin to cultivate friendships with their non-Christian neighbors. This proposal may seem modest, given the immense problem of religious intolerance in the world today. I believe, however, that interreligious friendships will bear fruit in ways we do not fully anticipate today.

Friendship is by no means a new topic for Christians. At the Last Supper, according to the Gospel of John, Jesus took an unusual step for a first-century rabbi: he addressed his disciples not as slaves but as friends (Jn 15:13–15). In Christian tradition, the understanding of friendship and what these friendships might mean for us spiritually was shaped largely by the need to understand the relationship between two different forms of love, *philia* and *agapé*.

Philia is preferential love, the form of love that Aristotle wrote of at length. *Philia* is "preferential" in that we are friendly with some and not with others because we see in the friend qualities that we find appealing or preferable to other qualities. In contrast to Aristotle's preferential form of love, *agapé* is the unconditional love preached by Jesus. Like the love of the father in Jesus' story of the Prodigal Son, *agapé* is steadfast, unwavering, and constant. *Philia* is self-serving in that we generally choose to be friendly with those who can be of benefit to us or who please us. *Agapē* is not a matter of choice. Unconditional love is Jesus' command to his disciples. Thus, *agapē* is to be shown not only to the friend but to the enemy as well. Distinguishing between these two forms of love is useful in coming to insight about friendships, including friendships with people who follow a religious path different from one's own. We may love someone who hates us, but try as we might, we cannot be friends with them. *Philia* is not only preferential; it is also reciprocal. *Agapē* is the more radical form of love, an unconditional command that applies whether we find the character in question appealing or not.

In Christian tradition, *agapē* has eclipsed *philia*. Aristotle's preferential love has not been dismissed as evil. *Philia*, rather, has been seen as inferior and auxiliary to *agapē*, which is the perfection of love. Here I want to suggest that those interested in doing theology comparatively should think again about *philia*. Christians should always look upon their non-Christian neighbors mindful of Jesus' unconditional command to love. Each and every human being, regardless of religious beliefs, is precious in the eyes of God. Perhaps *agapē* can be seen as the guiding force behind all three of the candidates for a theology of religions. This is easily seen in Rahner's inclusivist theology of the anonymous Christian. The God of Jesus Christ loves each and every human being with a love that becomes concrete and tangible in any number of ways, including the religious lives of Buddhists and Hindus, Confucians and Muslims, Jews and Jains. In compliance with Jesus' command to love, Christians are required to see the Holy Spirit at work in the many religions of the world.[8] *Agapē* seems to be a factor at work among the pluralist theologians as well. John Hick's call for religious tolerance has been criticized as a form of modern Western secular humanism. Although Hick's starting presuppositions are more philosophical than religious, his call to resist religious fanaticism and tolerate all religions has deep roots in his own commitments as a Christian believer.[9] Certainly Jesus' command to love is evident in Paul Knitter's attempt to bring together a pluralist theology of religions with Christianity's struggle for social justice.

If Jesus' command to love leads Christians to the need to develop a theology of religions, *philia* helps Christians to do theology comparatively. *Agapē* requires Christians to love the non-Christian regardless of their actual beliefs and religious practices. *Philia*, which is preferential love, calls Christians to enter into friendships with non-Christians based on the innate attractiveness of their actual beliefs and religious practices. In other words, Christians should hold non-Christians in friendship based on a preferential love, a love that treasures the non-Christian not because of Jesus' command to love, but because of the innate goodness and virtue of the friend. Of course, I do not mean to suggest that Christians should abandon *agapē* in favor of *philia*. However, if Christians think about their non-Christian neighbors only in terms of *agapē*, moving beyond the theology of religions to comparative theology will be difficult. As a practical matter, complementing our unconditional love of non-Christians with a preferential love will enable us to befriend non-Christians for their own sake. Such interreligious friendships offer an invaluable setting for doing theology comparatively.

All our friends, even our oldest and most valued friends, were once strangers to us. Entering into new friendships requires us to make room in our lives for what is foreign and unknown. This is all the more the case when the stranger we befriend follows a religious path different from our own. If interreligious friendships provide a practical context for Christians who want to do theology comparatively, then we need to reflect more concretely on the value of friendships that reach across religious traditions.

Befriending a stranger can be beneficial in numerous ways. Being too comfortable with our lives is a risk we all run. To surround ourselves with what is familiar, tried, and true seems only natural. Security, however, can also become stifling. Making new friends requires us to step out of our security and enter into a less comfortable world where the unpredictable replaces the tried and true. Befriending a stranger exposes us to a world of ideas and experiences that is not our own. Of course, this can be scary, but sometimes the *stranger* is the one who rescues us from our stubborn preoccupation with ourselves and our overly settled lives. If the stranger is the one who shatters our autonomy and security, the stranger is also the one who liberates us from our self-absorption. This is all the more the case when the stranger we befriend leads a life rooted in religious beliefs and practices that are not our own. The non-Christian believer comes to us with stories that we have never heard before, with questions we have not asked, ways of responding to life that we have not imagined. New stories, new questions, and new customs, by expanding our horizons, allow us to see ourselves and our own religious tradition in new ways. In this respect, interreligious friendships can be destabilizing, but also empowering. The stranger poses a threat to our current self-understanding, but also brings with her the power to liberate us for understanding ourselves as Christians in new and welcome ways.

To be threatened by what is strange, unforeseen, or foreign is no doubt a natural human response. The long and sad history of religious intolerance gives ample support for this conclusion. In Christian history, the stranger's religion has been demonized as terrorism, ridiculed as superstition, dismissed as heathen, or neutralized by sophisticated theological methods. All the theologies of religions provide strategies for inoculating ourselves against the threat of the stranger. For Barth, the stranger's religion is merely a human creation that cannot be compared with Christianity, to which has been given God's incomparable revelation. For Rahner, at the depths of the stranger's religion we will discover what is already familiar to us, Christ. The pluralists argue, each in his or her own way, that the stranger is not really a threat to us, because the differences that separate us are not of real consequence. In each case, not only the strangeness but also the power and danger of other religious traditions are neutralized.

Interreligious friendships help Christians to resist the tendency to fear what is strange. Overcoming this fear is essential if we are to do theology comparatively. In order to befriend the religious stranger, we must confront our fear of what is strange and live with the ambiguities of a world of vast religious diversity. In interreligious friendships, non-Christian religions become living realities for Christian believers. Of course, in doing theology comparatively, Christians can learn much about other religions by reading books. In interreligious friendships, however, the friend's religion becomes a living reality, no longer confined to the pages of the book, an embodied truth, not an abstract doctrine. Christianity exists not in books but rather in the actual lives of Christian believers. The same is true of all religions.

In interreligious friendships, truths foreign to my own religious convictions become living realities and real possibilities for shaping my religious beliefs and giving new direction to my religious life. Such friendships provide a helpful context for confronting one's fear of the stranger and thus offer a good way to begin to do theology comparatively. Truths from outside my tradition become theological resources that empower my own religious quest to discover the depths of my own tradition. Interreligious friendships, however, are valuable in another way as well. Often our disagreements with our friends are more honest and more truthful, and thus better, than our disagreements with total strangers. To disagree with the Buddhist understanding of God in general is one thing. To disagree with your Buddhist friend's understanding of God is rather different. In an interreligious friendship, differences in belief are never abstract. Real religious practitioners have made really different commitments with serious implications for life. To be able to differ honestly with another human being on matters of ultimate importance must be counted an achievement. Friendship makes that achievement all the more impressive. In order to do theology comparatively, Christians will do well to develop deep and abiding friendships with their non-Christian neighbors as a useful way to disagree with honesty and depth.

Although interreligious friendships are not easy, they are by no means unprecedented. For example, in July 1996, Buddhist and Roman Catholic monks and nuns gathered at the Trappist monastery at Gethsemani, Kentucky. Many of these Buddhists and Christians were old friends. For some years now, Catholics and Buddhists have been opening up their monasteries to one another in friendship. In sharing their religious lives and cherished beliefs, the Buddhists have been very skillful in inspiring their Christian friends to think about prayer and meditation, sin and transcendence, Christ and the monastic life in new and creative ways. Poignantly, the Dalai Lama proposed Gethsemani, a Catholic monastery, as a fitting site for this meeting of friends because he wished to place a Tibetan prayer shawl over the simple cross that marks the grave of Thomas Merton, his friend, buried beside the monastery chapel. Gustav Weigel, a Jesuit priest, spent his last night on earth with his old and dear friend, Rabbi Abraham Heschel. The Jew and the Christian passed the evening in quiet conversation sharing with one another their hopes and confessing their deficiencies. Rabbi Heschel's friend died a peaceful death after returning home that evening. For some eight years now, a group of Christians and Buddhists has been meeting in Los Angeles to learn from one another and deepen their own religious commitments. Before the dialogue begins, however, there is always lunch. Friendship is the basis for this dialogue, which has produced much fruit in the lives of all the participants.

Comparative Theology as an Act of Hope

Both of the examples of doing theology comparatively began with an act of hope on the part of a Christian believer: the meaning of Christianity can be embraced at a deeper level by using the insights of non-Christian religions as a resource. As a closing thought, I want to reflect on comparative theology as an act of Christian hope and the implications of this hope for Christian believers in a world of wondrous, if troubling, religious diversity.

Implicit in doing theology comparatively is a hope that Christianity's encounter with non-Christian religions can lead to a profound transformation in ourselves as a religious community of believers. A serious encounter with a non-Christian believer should not leave a Christian unchanged. Of course, change for its own sake is nothing praiseworthy, especially when we are dealing with matters as important as our religious commitments. However, given the challenge religious diversity poses to Christians today, learning how to be skillful in the theological art of changing our mind well should be counted a virtue.

Studying other religious traditions seriously on their own terms and entering into friendships with non-Christian believers will certainly help Christians to become skillful in the art of changing their minds well. In addition, Christians need to recognize more deeply than ever that their religious tradition changes. Doing theology comparatively presumes that Christian doctrine continues to develop. There are, of course, several views of how Christian teaching has developed over the centuries.[10] The findings of comparative theologians will no doubt contribute significantly to this discussion as well. Right now, however, the two exercises in comparison should make clear that comparative theology does not envision the abandonment of Christian belief, but rather its slow and careful transformation. In this respect, comparative theology must be seen as a form of Christianity's hope.

The hope that the meaning of Christianity can be embraced at a deeper level by using the insights of non-Christian religions as a resource will not always be fulfilled. Sometimes comparisons will yield only superficial similarities. At other times, comparisons will run up against insurmountable differences. In neither case can Christians expect to learn very much from their non-Christian neighbors. However, if our comparisons are made skillfully and based on increasing knowledge about non-Christian religions, I believe that most exercises in comparative theology will fall into the middle between these two extremes. Exercises in comparison will reveal both similarities and differences between Christianity and non-Christian religions. Both the similarities and the differences will be stimulating for Christians as they explore the meaning of their own religious beliefs comparatively.

The hope of comparative theology will come to fruition very slowly. This is the case for a number of reasons. Since comparative theology is *Christian* theology, it is necessarily a communal effort. Theology is not the pursuit of a solitary seeker. Comparative theology, like all theology, is part of the life of the Christian community, the church. Therefore, the comparison of Krishna and the *gopis* with the parable of the Prodigal Son needs to be repeated by other Christian believers and the results compared with my findings. Likewise, other Christian theologians need to read Dogen on the meaning of death and compare Buddhist teachings with Christian belief about the resurrection of the body. In repeating these experiments, other Christian believers may reach different conclusions than I did. In this case, a conversation that began between a Christian and a Buddhist thinker will have become a conversation among Christians about the meaning of their own tradition, but a theological conversation inspired by Buddhist wisdom. Slowly, a fabric of understanding will be established. No effort to compare can ever really be finished. This should be counted a strength, not a weakness, for comparative theology.

There is another reason why comparative theology can only proceed slowly. Christianity will be transformed only through the transformation of Christian believers themselves. Here I am talking about a real deepening in our religious vision, a spiritual transformation generated by the encounter between the truths of Christianity and the truths of non-Christian religions. In this transformation, Christian believers will find a way to deal with religious diversity in a way that is responsible and creative, responsible to the demands of their own religious tradition and creative in looking on the greatness of other religious tradition as a way to plunge more deeply into the greatness of their own.

NOTES

1. Donald Mitchell, *Spirituality and Emptiness* (New York: Paulist Press, 1991); John Cobb, *Beyond Dialogue* (Philadelphia: Fortress Press, 1982); Leo Lefebure, *The Buddha and the Christ: Explorations in Buddhist and Christian Dialogue* (Maryknoll, N.Y.: Orbis Books, 1993); John Keenan, *The Meaning of Christ—a Mahayana Christology* (Maryknoll, N.Y.: Orbis Books, 1989); idem, *A Mahayana Reading of the Gospel of Mark* (Maryknoll, N.Y.: Orbis Books, 1995); Francis X. Clooney, *Theology After Vedanta* (Albany, N.Y.: SUNY Press, 1993); idem, *Seeing Through Texts* (Albany, N.Y.: SUNY Press, 1996); David Carpenter, *Revelation, History, and the Dialogue of Religions: A Comparative Study of Bhartrhari and Bonaventure* (Maryknoll, N.Y.: Orbis Books, 1995); John Berthrong, *All Under Heaven: Transforming Paradigms in Confucian-Christian Dialogue* (Albany, N.Y.: SUNY Press, 1994); David Burrell, *Knowing the Unknowable God: Ibn-Sina, Maimonides, Aquinas* (Notre Dame, Ind.: University of Notre Dame Press, 1986); idem, *Freedom and Creation in Three Traditions* (Notre Dame, Ind.: University of Notre Dame Press, 1993).

2. Francis X. Clooney, S.J., "The Study of Non-Christian Religions in the Post-Vatican II Roman Catholic Church," *Journal of Ecumenical Studies* 28, no. 3 (1991): 487.

3. Clooney, *Theology After Vedanta*, 4–6.

4. Diana Eck, "The Mosque Next Door," *Harvard Magazine*, Sept.-Oct. 1996, pp. 38–44. See also the web site for the Harvard University Pluralism Project, pluralism@fas.harvard.edu.

5. Eck, "The Mosque Next Door," 44.

6. Karl Barth, *Church Dogmatics* 1/2, ed. G. W. Bromiley and T. F. Torrance (Edinburgh: T. & T. Clark, 1956), 299.

7. Eck, "The Mosque Next Door," 44.

8. See, for example, Karl Rahner, "Christianity and the Non-Christian Religions," in *Theological Investigations* V (Baltimore, Md.: Helicon Press, 1966), 115–34.

9. For Hick's own account of his "spiritual pilgrimage," see *God Has Many Names: Britain's New Religious Pluralism* (London: Macmillan, 1980), 1–9.

10. For a useful summary of the various questions regarding the development of doctrine, see William Reiser, S.J., *What Are They Saying About Dogma?* (New York: Paulist Press, 1978).

180

SELECT BIBLIOGRAPHY

Barth, Karl. *Church Dogmatics* 1/2. Edited by G. W. Bromiley and T. F. Torrance, 297–327. Edinburgh: T. & T. Clark, 1956.

Berthrong, John. *All Under Heaven: Transforming Paradigms in Confucian–Christian Dialogue*. Albany, N.Y.: SUNY Press, 1994.

Boutin, Maurice. "Anonymous Christianity: A Paradigm for Interreligious Encounter?" *Journal of Ecumenical Studies* 20, no. 4 (1983): 602–29.

Braaten, Karl. *No Other Gospel! Christianity Among the World's Religions*. Minneapolis: Fortress Press, 1992.

———. "The Uniqueness and Universality of Jesus Christ." In *Christ's Lordship and Religious Pluralism*, edited by Gerald H. Andersen and Thomas F. Stransky, C.S.P. Maryknoll, N.Y.: Orbis Books, 1981.

Bracken, Joseph. *The Divine Matrix: Creativity as Link Between East and West*. Maryknoll, N.Y.: Orbis Books, 1995.

Burrell, David. *Freedom and Creation in Three Traditions*. Notre Dame, Ind.: University of Notre Dame Press, 1993.

———. *Knowing the Unknowable God: Ibn-Sina, Maimonides, Aquinas*. Notre Dame, Ind.: University of Notre Dame Press, 1986.

Carman, John. *Majesty and Meekness: A Comparative Study of Contrast and Harmony in the Concept of God*. Grand Rapids: William B. Eerdmans, 1991.

Carpenter, David. *Revelation, History, and the Dialogue of Religions: A Comparative Study of Bhartrhari and Bonaventure*. Maryknoll, N.Y.: Orbis Books, 1995.

Clooney, Francis X. *Seeing Through Texts*. Albany, N.Y.: SUNY Press, 1996.

———. "The Study of Non-Christian Religions in the Post–Vatican II Roman Catholic Church." *Journal of Ecumenical Studies* 28, no. 3 (1991): 482–94.

————. *Theology After Vedanta*. Albany, N.Y.: SUNY Press, 1993.

Cobb, John B. *Beyond Dialogue*. Philadelphia: Fortress Press, 1982.

————. "Beyond Pluralism." In *Christian Uniqueness Reconsidered: The Myth of a Pluralistic Theology of Religions*, edited by Gavin D'Costa. Maryknoll, N.Y.: Orbis Books, 1990.

————. "The Meaning of Pluralism in Christian Self-Understanding." In *Religious Pluralism,* edited by Leroy Rouner. Notre Dame, Ind.: University of Notre Dame Press, 1984.

Cornille, Catherine, and Valeer Neckerbrouck. *A Universal Faith?* Louvain: Peeters, 1992.

D'Costa, Gavin. *Theology and Religious Pluralism: The Challenge of Other Religions*. Oxford: Basil Blackwell, 1985.

D'Costa, Gavin, ed. *Christian Uniqueness Reconsidered: The Myth of a Pluralistic Theology of Religions*. Maryknoll, N.Y.: Orbis Books, 1990.

Dean, Thomas. "The Conflict of Christologies: A Response to S. Mark Heim." *Journal of Ecumenical Studies* 24 (Spring 1987): 24–31.

de Lubac, Henri. *Paradox et Mystère de l'Eglise*. Paris: Editions du Cerf, 1967.

Dinoia, Joseph. *The Diversity of Religions: A Christian Perspective*. Washington, D.C.: The Catholic University of America Press, 1992.

Driver, Thomas. "The Case for Pluralism." In *The Myth of Christian Uniqueness: Toward a Pluralistic Theology of Religions*, edited by John Hick and Paul Knitter. Maryknoll, N.Y.: Orbis Books, 1987.

Dupuis, Jacques, *Jesus Christ at the Encounter of World Religions*. Translated by Robert R. Barr. Maryknoll, N.Y.: Orbis Books, 1991.

Eck, Diana. *Encountering God: A Spiritual Journey from Bozeman to Banaras*. Boston: Beacon Press, 1993.

Fredericks, James. "A Universal Religious Experience?" *Horizons, Journal of the College Theology Society* 22, no. 1 (Spring 1995): 67–87.

Gilkey, Langdon. "Plurality and its Theological Implications." In *The Myth of Christian Uniqueness: Toward a Pluralistic Theology of Religions*, edited by John Hick and Paul Knitter. Maryknoll, N.Y.: Orbis Books, 1987.

————. "A Theological Voyage with Wilfred Cantwell Smith." *Religious Studies Review* 7, no. 4 (October 1981): 298–306.

Griffith, Paul. *An Apology for Apologetics: A Study in the Logic of Interreligious Dialogue*. Maryknoll, N.Y.: Orbis Books, 1991.

————. "The Uniqueness of Christian Doctrine Defended." In *Christian Uniqueness Reconsidered: The Myth of a Pluralistic Theology of Religions*, edited by Gavin D'Costa. Maryknoll, N.Y.: Orbis Books, 1990.

Habito, Ruben. *Healing Breath*. Maryknoll, N.Y.: Orbis Books, 1989.

————. *Total Liberation*. Maryknoll, N.Y.: Orbis Books, 1989.

Heim, S. Mark. *Is Christ the Only Way? Christian Faith in a Pluralistic World*. Valley Forge, Penn.: Judson Press, 1985.

————. *Salvations: Truth and Difference in Religion*. Maryknoll, N.Y.: Orbis Books, 1995.

————. "Thinking About Theocentric Christology." *Journal of Ecumenical Studies* 24 (Spring 1987): 1–16.

Hick, John. *A Christian Theology of Religions: The Rainbow of Faiths*. Louisville, Ky.: Westminster John Knox Press, 1995.

————. *God and the Universe of Faiths*. New York: St. Martin's Press, 1973.

————. *God Has Many Names: Britain's New Religious Pluralism*. London: Macmillan, 1980.

————. *An Interpretation of Religion: Human Responses to the Transcendent*. New Haven: Yale University Press, 1989.

————. "Jesus and the World Religions." In *The Myth of God Incarnate*, edited by John Hick and Paul Knitter. Philadelphia: Westminster Press, 1977.

————. *The Metaphor of God Incarnate*. London: SCM Press, 1993.

————. "The Non-Absoluteness of Christianity." In *The Myth of Christian Uniqueness: Toward a Pluralistic Theology of Religions*, edited by John Hick and Paul Knitter. Maryknoll, N.Y.: Orbis Books, 1987.

————. "On Grading Religions." *Religious Studies* 17 (1981): 451–67.

————. *Problems of Religious Pluralism*. New York: St. Martin's Press, 1985.

————. "Whatever Path Men Choose is Mine." In *Christianity and the Other Religions*, edited by John Hick and Brian Hebblethwaite. Philadelphia: Fortress Press, 1980.

Hick, John, and Brian Hebblethwaite, eds. *Christianity and the Other Religions*. Philadelphia: Fortress Press, 1980.

Hick, John, and Paul Knitter, eds. *The Myth of Christian Uniqueness: Toward a Pluralistic Theology of Religions*. Maryknoll, N.Y.: Orbis Books, 1987.

Jathana, Constantine, ed. *Dialogue in Community: Essays in Honor of Stanley J. Samartha*. Mangalore, India: Karnataka Theological Research Institute, 1982.

Keenan, John. *A Mahayana Reading of the Gospel of Mark*. Maryknoll, N.Y.: Orbis Books, 1995.

————. *The Meaning of Christ—A Mahayana Christology*. Maryknoll, N.Y.: Orbis Books, 1989.

Knitter, Paul. "Beyond a Monoreligious Theological Education." In *Shifting Boundaries: Contextual Approaches to the Structure of Theological*

Education, edited by Barbara G. Wheeler and Edward Farley. Louisville: Westminster/John Knox Press, 1991.

————. "Dialogue and Liberation: Foundations for a Pluralistic Theology of Religions." *The Drew Gateway* 58 (1988): 1–53.

————. "Five Theses Regarding the Uniqueness of Jesus." In *The Uniqueness of Jesus: A Dialogue with Paul F. Knitter*, edited by Leonard Swidler and Paul Mojzes. Maryknoll, N.Y.: Orbis Books, 1997.

————. *Jesus and the Other Names: Christian Mission and Global Responsibility*. Maryknoll, N.Y.: Orbis Books, 1996.

————. *No Other Name? A Critical Survey of Christian Attitudes Toward the World Religions*. Maryknoll, N.Y.: Orbis Books, 1985.

————. *One Earth Many Religions: Multifaith Dialogue and Global Responsibility*. Maryknoll, N.Y.: Orbis Books, 1995.

————. "Toward a Liberationist Theology of Religions." In *The Myth of Christian Uniqueness*, edited by John Hick and Paul Knitter. Maryknoll, N.Y.: Orbis Books, 1987.

Kraemer, Hendrick. *The Christian Message in a Non-Christian World*. London: Harper & Brothers, 1938.

Krieger, David. *The New Universalism: Foundations for a Global Theology*. Maryknoll, N.Y.: Orbis Books, 1991.

Lefebure, Leo. *The Buddha and the Christ: Explorations in Buddhist and Christian Dialogue*. Maryknoll, N.Y.: Orbis Books, 1993.

Loya, Joseph, Wan-li Ho, and Chang-Shin Jih. *The Tao of Jesus: An Experiment in Inter-Traditional Understanding*. Mahwah, N.J.: Paulist Press, 1998.

Mitchell, Donald. *Spirituality and Emptiness*. New York: Paulist Press, 1991.

Neville, Robert C. *Behind the Masks of God: An Essay Toward Comparative Theology*. Albany, N.Y.: SUNY Press, 1991.

Novak, David. *Jewish-Christian Dialogue: A Jewish Justification*. New York: Oxford University Press, 1989.

Ogden, Shubert. *Is There One True Religion or Are There Many?* Dallas: Southern Methodist University Press, 1992.

Panikkar, Raymundo. *The Intrareligious Dialogue*. New York: Paulist Press, 1978.

————. "The Jordan, the Tiber and the Ganges: Three Kairological Moments of Christic Self-Consciousness." In *The Myth of Christian Uniqueness: Toward a Pluralistic Theology of Religions*, edited by John Hick and Paul Knitter. Maryknoll, N.Y.: Orbis Books, 1987.

————. *The Unknown Christ of Hinduism*. Maryknoll, N.Y.: Orbis Books, 1981.

Pannenberg, Wolfhart. "Religious Pluralism and Conflicting Truth Claims: The Problem of a Theology of the World Religions." In *Christian Uniqueness Reconsidered: The Myth of a Pluralistic Theology of Religions*, edited by Gavin D'Costa. Maryknoll, N.Y.: Orbis Books, 1990.

Perry, Edmund, and N. Ross Reat. *A World Theology: The Central Spiritual Reality of Humankind*. New York: Cambridge University Press, 1991.

Race, Alan. *Christians and Religious Pluralism: Patterns in the Christian Theology of Religions*. Maryknoll, N.Y.: Orbis Books, 1982.

Rahner, Karl. "Anonymous and Explicit Faith." In *Theological Investigations* XVI. New York: Crossroad, 1966.

_____. "Anonymous Christianity and the Missionary Task of the Church." In *Theological Investigations* XII. New York: Seabury, 1974.

_____. "Atheism and Implicit Christianity." In *Theological Investigations* IX. New York: Herder and Herder, 1972.

_____. "Christianity and the Non-Christian Religions." In *Theological Investigations* V. Baltimore, Md.: Helicon Press, 1966.

_____. "Observations on the Problem of the 'Anonymous Christian.'" In *Theological Investigations* XIV. New York: Seabury, 1976.

_____. "The One Christ and the Universality of Salvation." *Theological Investigations* XVI. New York: Crossroad, 1979.

Rouner, Leroy, ed. *Religious Pluralism*. Notre Dame, Ind.: University of Notre Dame Press, 1984.

Samartha, Stanley J. *Courage for Dialogue: Ecumenical Issues in Interreligious Relationships*. Maryknoll, N.Y.: Orbis Books, 1982.

_____. "The Cross and the Rainbow: Christ in a Multi-religious Culture." In *The Myth of Christian Uniqueness: Toward a Pluralistic Theology of Religions*, edited by John Hick and Paul Knitter. Maryknoll, N.Y.: Orbis Books, 1987.

_____. "Dialogue as a Continuing Christian Concern." In *Living Faiths and the Ecumenical Movement*. Geneva: WCC, 1971. Reprinted in *Christianity and the Other Religions*, edited by John Hick and Brian Hebblethwaite. Philadelphia: Fortress Press, 1980.

_____. *The Hindu Response to the Unbound Christ*. Bangalore: Christian Institute for the Study of Religion and Society, 1974.

_____. "The Lordship of Jesus Christ and Religious Pluralism." In *Christ's Lordship and Religious Pluralism*, edited by Gerald H. Anderson and Thomas F. Stransky, C.S.P. Maryknoll, N.Y.: Orbis Books, 1981.

_____. *One Christ—Many Religions: Toward a Revised Christology*. Maryknoll, N.Y.: Orbis Books, 1991.

Smith, Wilfred Cantwell. *Faith and Belief*. Princeton: Princeton University Press, 1979.

_____. "Idolatry in Comparative Perspective." In *The Myth of Christian Uniqueness: Toward a Pluralistic Theology of Religions*, edited by John Hick and Paul Knitter. Maryknoll, N.Y.: Orbis Books, 1987.

_____. *Toward a World Theology*. Philadelphia: Westminster Press, 1981.

_____. *What Is Scripture? A Comparative Approach*. Minneapolis: Fortress Press, 1993.

Sullivan, Francis. *Salvation Outside the Church?* Mahwah, N.J.: Paulist Press, 1992.

Thangaraj, M. T. *The Crucified Guru: An Experiment in Cross-cultural Christology*. Nashville: Abingdon Press, 1994.

Tracy, David. *Dialogue with the Other: The Interreligious Dialogue*. Louvain: Peeter; Grand Rapids: William B. Eerdmans, 1990.

_____. "Comparative Theology." In *Encyclopedia of Religion*, 14:446–55. New York: Macmillan, 1987.

Vempeny, Ishanand. *Krsna and Christ: In the Light of Some of the Fundamental Concepts and Themes of the Bhagavad Gita and the New Testament*. Anand, India: Gujarat Sahitya Prakash; Prune: Ishvani Kendra, 1988.

von Bruck, Michael. *The Unity of Reality: God, God-Experience and Meditation in the Hindu-Christian Dialogue*. New York: Paulist Press, 1991.

Williamson, Clark. *A Guest in the House of Israel: Post-Holocaust Church Theology*. Louisville: Westminster/John Knox, 1993.

Yearley, L. *Aquinas and Mencius: Theories of Virtue and Concepts of Courage*. Albany, N.Y.: SUNY Press, 1990.

INDEX

Abe, Masao, 149–50
agapē, 173–75
anonymous Christian, 24–27,29–33
Aristotle, 173–74
ars moriendi, 156–57
avatar, 145

Barth, Karl, 16–22, 89, 90, 170,
    172, 176

Christianity, 18–19, 24–25
comparative theology, 8–10,
    139–40, 162–80
Copernican revolution, 38–39

de Lubac, Henri, 30–31
dialogue, 73, 115–16, 125–26, 133
Dinoia, Joseph, 162
Dogen, 146–49, 168

Eck, Diana, 12, 171–73
exclusivism, 6–7, 14-15, 16–22,
    87–89, 170

faith, 80, 81–83, 129
friendships, 173–77

gopis, 140–45, 168

Heim, S. Mark, 108
Hick, John, 37–53, 104–8, 109–10,
    114
hope, 178

idolatry, 87–89
inclusivism, 7, 15, 22–33, 38–39,
    87–89, 170–71
incarnation, 40–44, 59–60, 74–75,
    87, 90–92, 120–27, 145–46
intolerance, 1–3

Jesus Christ, 56–63, 74–76, 91–92,
    120–21

Kant, Immanuel, 45–46
Knitter, Paul, 55–76, 119–38
Krishna, 140–46, 168
Kung, Hans, 30

Liberal Protestantism, 121–22
liberation theology, 65–69,
    70–73, 127–35